JAMES MADISON

PRESIDENTIAL ✦ LEADERS

JAMES MADISON

JEREMY ROBERTS

LERNER PUBLICATIONS COMPANY/MINNEAPOLIS

For my friends at the Chester Library, who never knew how much they helped

Lerner Publications Company
A division of Lerner Publishing Group
241 First Avenue North
Minneapolis, MN 55401 U.S.A.

Website address: www.lernerbooks.com

Library of Congress Cataloging-in-Publication Data

Roberts, Jeremy, 1956–
    James Madison / by Jeremy Roberts.
        p.   cm. — (Presidential leaders)
    Summary: A biography of the fourth president of the United States, who helped ensure ratification of the Constitution and the Bill of Rights. Includes bibliographical references (p.   ) and index.
    ISBN: 0–8225–0823–0 (lib. bdg. : alk. paper)
    1. Madison, James, 1751–1836—Juvenile literature. 2. Presidents—United States—Biography—Juvenile literature. [1. Madison, James, 1751–1836. 2. Presidents.] I. Title. II. Series.
E342.R63 2004
973.5'1'092—dc22   2003019976

Manufactured in the United States of America
1 2 3 4 5 6 – JR – 09 08 07 06 05 04

Contents

———— ✧ ————

INTRODUCTION: IN FULL FLIGHT..................................7

1 **SMALL BEGINNINGS**..............................9

2 **REVOLUTION**....................................21

3 **A NEW CONSTITUTION**...........................33

4 **LION OF THE HOUSE**............................45

5 **LOVE AND HATE**................................62

6 **SECRETARY OF STATE**...........................77

7 **WAR ON THE HORIZON**...........................87

8 **TRIUMPH AT LAST**..............................96

TIMELINE...104

SOURCE NOTES...106

SELECTED BIBLIOGRAPHY..................................107

FURTHER READING, WEBSITES, AND VIDEOS........108

INDEX..110

During the War of 1812, President James Madison did what he could to help U.S. troops set up defenses around Washington, D.C. The city was burned, but the ideals of democracy remained as strong as ever, and the capital was quickly rebuilt.

IN FULL FLIGHT

*"It is my good fortune . . . to have the path
in which I am to tread, lighted by examples
of illustrious services."*
—James Madison, First Inaugural Address, 1809

President James Madison struggled to control his excited horse on the hills just south of Washington, D.C. A short distance away, hundreds of British soldiers were marching forward, aiming to sack and destroy the city.

A little over a decade after the Revolutionary War, the United States was once again at war with Great Britain. American troops worked feverishly to set up defenses, but their generals were mostly inept. Madison did what he could to help. As British rockets began flaring nearby, it was clear that Madison could not stay here. The future of the country depended on its president escaping the battle unharmed. Reluctantly, he steadied his horse and retreated to another line of defense, the last between the enemy and the city of Washington itself.

A few miles away, Madison's wife Dolley ran through the presidential mansion, desperately gathering the government's important papers. Messengers covered with the dirt of battle urged her to leave. But Dolley refused. Her husband had said he would return, and she wanted to wait for him. Finally, a friend dragged her from the house—but not before she set out dinner for her husband and saved a portrait of the nation's first president, George Washington.

Below the city, the British advanced mercilessly. Everywhere was confusion and chaos. President Madison stood on the hill, worrying about his country's future. Would the great experiment in democracy survive? Would the government he had helped design live to fight another day?

The booming cannons and the darkening sky held little hope, but Madison refused to despair. He climbed on his horse and did what he could to stop the retreating American soldiers, trying to rally them to the defense. Though Madison was short in height, his character towered over the battle, his voice hoarse as he tried to rally his troops.

In the end, Madison would not be able to stop the British attack. But he and the country he served would quickly recover from it. And the beliefs and ideals that the president had championed would shine stronger than ever.

CHAPTER ONE

SMALL BEGINNINGS

*"I am too dull . . . to look out for any
extraordinary things in this world. . . . "*
—James Madison, to his friend William Bradford

John Maddison walked toward the side of the ship as it
approached the Virginia coast. He gazed out at the
looming docks. The city before him was still small, certainly compared to any in England in the 1600s. But as
one of the fastest growing settlements in Britain's
American colonies, it was full of promise. In England a
skilled carpenter like John might earn a decent living.
But in the wilderness beyond the settled shore, a hard-
working, intelligent man could rise far beyond his hum-
ble middle-class roots.

Land was cheap in the Virginia colony. If you paid for
the passage of twelve people across the Atlantic—as John
had done—you were entitled to six hundred acres, free and
clear. Of course, you had to chop down the trees, build the

Life in the early colonies was lonely and often involved intense labor.

farm buildings, and maybe even make the road leading to them. But in 1653, Virginia was a good route to fortune for a man like John.

It could also lead to starvation and early death. The outcome depended as much on luck as your own hard work.

For the next three decades, John Maddison, James Madison's great-great-grandfather, expanded his holdings. Eventually, he owned about 1,900 acres in the area of the York and Mattaponi Rivers in Virginia. The family continued to grow and acquire land in Virginia. Gradually, they moved westward, helping to tame what was then forest. Among John's great-grandchildren was James Madison Sr. (By then the family had dropped the second "d.") James Sr.

began running the family plantation around the time he turned eighteen in 1741. He married Nellie Conway. Their first son, James Jr., the future president, was born at midnight March 16, 1751.

Young James's family was well-off by the standards of the day. While he remembered the Madisons as "respectable but not opulent [rich]," they were very powerful and important in their community. James's father served as a church vestryman, an important position in early Virginia. He was also sheriff and then judge. Wealth and power were usually measured in terms of land ownership, and the family had a very large and productive plantation that by 1754 measured just under four thousand acres.

Large plantations such as the Madisons' needed many workers to keep it running smoothly. Theirs employed nearly one hundred slaves.

James Madison Sr. held important positions in his Virginia community, including sheriff and judge.

———————— ✧

In those days, large plantations were like miniature villages. Besides the family and servants, roughly one hundred slaves lived on the Madison plantation during James's youth. Barns and other buildings for animals were clustered on the property. From the time he was about nine years old, the center of the plantation was a large house known as Montpelier.

James Sr. and Nellie filled their house with a large family. Three children died in childbirth, and two others died very young, leaving seven to grow to adulthood. Francis (1753) and Ambrose (1755) were closest to James in age. Later came William (1762) and three sisters—Nelly (1760), Sarah (1764), and Frances, or Fanny (1774).

SCHOOLING

Details of James Jr.'s early education are lost, but it was common at the time for children to learn to read and write at home. Historians believe that his grandmother, Frances Taylor Madison, who lived with the family, may have helped educate him. His father's library contained eighty-five books, a good number in those days. The young Madison probably read all of them as he grew.

In 1762 eleven-year-old James left home to study with Donald Robertson, a well known teacher in King and Queen County. Here James's studies probably included Latin and Greek, the ancient languages of classic literature. At the time, learning these languages was an important first step toward learning advanced logic, philosophy, and even science. He also learned astronomy, geometry, and many other subjects. He greatly admired his teacher and was proud of his early education. Both laid the foundation for his later learning. "All that I have been in life I owe largely to that man," he said later of Robertson.

COLLEGE AND RELIGION

Most well-to-do Virginia families at the time sent their sons to William and Mary College at Williamsburg, Virginia. However, James chose to go to the College of New Jersey, which was later renamed Princeton. A tutor who prepared James for higher education had gone to the college and highly recommended it. New Jersey's climate was also thought to be healthier than Virginia's damp heat.

James and his family may have also chosen the college because of its reputation for encouraging religious liberty, or freedom. In Great Britain, the government supported the Church of England. All other religions were restricted, and at times, their followers were persecuted. This was true in Virginia as well.

The Madisons belonged to the Church of England. But James's father was not a passionate supporter of the Church and may even have disagreed with some of its leaders.

William and Mary College was closely connected to the Church of England. The Madisons probably felt the college would not encourage freethinking (forming opinions based on reason instead of religious authority) or allow James to get a wide-ranging education.

NEW JERSEY

The thick, red dust from the roadbed flew up everywhere as James Madison rode northward from Virginia to New Jersey in the late summer of 1769. The summer drought had ruined many crops and harmed his own family's finances. But young James's thoughts lay beyond the fields and forests of his youth. His destination was a stone building called Nassau

————————————— ✧ —————————————

Madison attended many classes in Nassau Hall, which was at the heart of the College of New Jersey.

Hall, the center of the college and the small town around it. Though founded only twenty-three years before, the school was already well known in the colonies, thanks partly to its president, Dr. John Witherspoon. Witherspoon railed against the Church of England's power. He advocated freedom of religion, which at the time mostly meant freedom to practice different Christian religions.

James quickly threw himself into his studies. His classes emphasized the classics, many borrowed from

John Witherspoon

Dr. Witherspoon's personal library. James's love for religious liberty and freethinking grew quickly, and he soon joined a group on campus known as the American Whig Society. Like other members of the group, he became interested in politics and the growing debate over what role the king and government of Great Britain should play in governing the colonies.

Some of the debate was about the role of religion and whether people should be free to worship as they pleased. But British laws concerning the colonies, such as the Stamp Act of 1765, were more hotly debated. The Stamp Act placed a tax on official documents, as well as on newspapers, cards, and even dice. Many people in America opposed the tax.

MADISON THE POET?

We remember James Madison as the main author of the Constitution, but at Princeton he was known for writing poetic satires. These were witty, humorous poems.

Most of James's satires commemorated fights between two groups of students on campus, the Whigs and the Tories. In the politics of the day, the Whigs were liberals who favored individual rights and freedoms. Tories were more conservative, seeking to preserve ties to Great Britain and loyalty to the king.

James was a Whig. His poems were often mildly vulgar. They were also boastful and usually clever, or at least intended to be. In the verse below, James compares the "noble Whigs" to Tories, who he jokingly calls sons of "owls, monkeys and baboons":

Come noble Whigs, disdain these sons
Of screech owls, monkeys and baboons.
Keep up your minds to humorous themes
And verdant mead[ow]s and flowing streams
Until this tribe of dunces find
The baseness of their groveling mind
And skulk within their dens together
Where each one's stench will kill his brother.

In Britain taxes were imposed by the people's elected representatives, or the Parliament. Through their representatives, citizens with the right to vote had a say in how they were taxed. But in America, colonists lost that right. Though they were still British subjects, they could not vote for members of Parliament. Their local governments had no say in passing laws such as the Stamp Act. Many colonists protested, saying this British policy was "taxation without representation." Though the Stamp Act had soon been repealed (withdrawn), the conflict remained: The British government needed to raise money to pay war debts and protect the colonies. Yet it would not allow the colonists to be represented in Parliament or give them the power to tax themselves.

James took great interest in the controversy and strongly sided with the colonial protesters. Witherspoon's son James proclaimed in a debate that "[citizens] are bound and obliged by the law of nature to resist their king, if he treats them cruelly or ignores the law of the state, and to defend their liberty." This was a radical idea at the time, but James Madison shared it fully.

"JEMMY"

While at college, Madison formed some close friendships. His friends knew him as "Jemmy." While he had a sometimes outrageous sense of humor, he shared it only in small groups and could turn very shy in a crowd. James was short, barely five-six, and skinny. He was not very athletic at all. He couldn't even speak loudly for too long before his squeaky, thin voice went hoarse.

At college James was thrown together with more than one hundred classmates from different colonies. For

twenty-one weeks each semester, he and the others lived
at Nassau Hall. Among his closest friends was William
Bradford, the son of a printer. Bradford eventually studied law and became one of the most important lawyers
in early America. Another friend was Philip Freneau,
known as the poet of the American Revolution. Among
his other classmates was Aaron Burr, who would eventually become an important political figure.

Hungry for ideas and knowledge, Madison devoted
himself to his studies as well as political debates among
the different student groups. After graduating in
September 1771, he put off the trip home for more than

—————————— ◇ ——————————

Madison met William Bradford (left) *and Philip Freneau* (right)
while studying at the College of New Jersey.

six months to study law and
Hebrew. His health also
delayed his return home. For
some time, he had been
stricken by mysterious fits
that kept him in bed for
long periods of time. James
said they were like "Epilepsy"
and were so severe that they
made it impossible for him
to study, let alone travel.
(Modern historians are not
quite sure what the illness
was.) The attacks would
plague him for the rest of his
life. There was no cure,
except rest.

Nelly Madison as an adult

When he reached home,
James began tutoring his younger brother William and
sisters Nelly and Sarah. As the oldest son, James could
expect to inherit the bulk of his father's farm. But he
had not yet settled on his own direction or a profession,
nor had he shown much interest in running the farm.
James's life seemed to be going nowhere.

In December 1773, news came of a protest in Boston
against a law called the Tea Act. The law all but forced
colonists to buy their tea from one British company. In
protest, some Bostonians snuck onto three ships carrying
British tea and dumped it all into Boston Harbor. Other
protests followed this event, later known as the Boston
Tea Party.

This painting depicts the citizens of Boston celebrating, as colonists dressed as Native Americans toss British tea into Boston Harbor.

———————————— ✧ ————————————

James followed the news of the protests closely. He thought it was wrong to destroy someone else's property. But he agreed with the radical, or extremist, colonists who argued that Americans needed greater freedom from Great Britain. Gradually, his belief in liberty began pushing him not only toward a career but toward a greater purpose in life.

CHAPTER TWO

REVOLUTION

"Religion . . . can be directed only by reason and conviction, not by force or violence."
—James Madison, explaining the Virginia
Declaration of Rights, 1776

James Madison was outraged. A Baptist preacher and some of his followers had been jailed for daring to preach without a government license in Culpepper County, not far from where Madison lived. The matter had been taken to the colony's lawmakers, who refused to protect the Baptists. Like most of the citizens of the colony, Baptists were Protestants. But their religious beliefs differed from those of the majority. The Baptists were not allowed to preach and were jailed when they tried to do so.

Madison told a friend this attack on religious freedom was nothing less than slavery. He used other strong words—"pride, ignorance, and knavery [misbehavior],"—to

Not all Protestants worshiped freely in the American colonies. Many Baptists, as well as members of other smaller religious groups, were prohibited from practicing their religious beliefs. Some hired guards (above) to protect them on their way to church.

denounce the leaders of the local Church of England. The Baptists' imprisonment convinced him more than ever that the government had no business telling people what religion they ought to follow.

At the same time, Madison connected the problems of religious freedom with the problems between the colonies and Great Britain. Many of the colonies had been started or populated by people who fled Great Britain to seek religious freedom. The present conflict over taxation was just one more attempt by the British government to dictate what the colonists could and could not do. It stripped them of the power to make decisions on their own.

PORT BILL

Madison visited former schoolmate William Bradford in Philadelphia, Pennsylvania, during the spring of 1774. While Madison was there, news arrived that the British Parliament had punished Boston for its Tea Party protest. Parliament had passed the Port Bill, which shut down all commerce, or business activities, in the port. The economic impact would be severe. Trade was not only the city's major industry, but many necessary goods could only come from overseas. Madison was furious. All he and many others

─────────── ✧ ───────────

Dozens of British warships dot Boston Harbor after Parliament passed the Port Bill. The port closing severely injured Boston's economy.

could talk about was the unjust cruelty of the British government. The Boston leaders sent a letter to the other colonies declaring that they had been treated harshly—and that the other colonies would soon be next. The leaders asked the other colonies to stop trading with Britain, hoping to pressure Parliament into changing its policies.

When he returned home from Philadelphia, Madison discovered many of his neighbors agreed with the idea of cutting off trade with Britain. "I find them very warm in favor," he wrote Bradford on July 1. Madison wanted more than just a repeal of the Port Bill. He wanted Parliament to state openly that Americans had the same rights and privileges that all British citizens had. No taxation without representation.

But Madison went even further, suggesting to Bradford that America should "begin our defense." In other words, he suggested that the colonists take military action if their rights were not recognized. He was calling for armed revolt. That sentiment ranked him with the most radical leaders in America.

Representatives from the colonies met to discuss the situation at the First Continental Congress in Philadelphia that fall. They voted to boycott, or ban, trade with Britain if the Boston Port Bill was not repealed. They also voted to establish committees, usually called "committees of safety," to enforce these boycotts in each county.

As a leading citizen, James Madison Sr. was a natural choice for the local county committee of safety. And as a young radical, his son James Jr. was an even more logical choice. Since only those who owned land could vote in a local election or hold office, James Jr. bought two hundred acres of his father's farm in September. On December 22,

1774, James and his father were among the fifteen members elected as the county committee.

James Sr., already a colonel in the local militia, or volunteer army, became chairman of the committee. Young James was among the small but growing minority who believed war was inevitable. His health remained fragile, but he practiced with the militia anyway.

The younger Madison was a devoted member of the committee. When a preacher refused to follow the committee's directions, Madison and the other committeemen threatened him and called him a traitor. The minister changed his ways. Had he not, Madison was ready to apply one of the common punishments of the time—pouring hot tar over him and covering him with feathers before parading him in disgrace through the town.

TOWARD INDEPENDENCE

In April 1775, a British force under Lieutenant General Thomas Gage attempted to seize American weapons in the Massachusetts towns of Lexington and Concord. The

—————————— ✧

Tarring and feathering as a punishment comes from medieval Europe (500s–1500s). Not only was it humiliating, but it was extremely painful as well.

troops came under fire from American minutemen, volunteer soldiers who opposed the strict British measures. (They got their name because they promised to be ready for a battle within sixty seconds.) The battles at Lexington and Concord ignited conflicts throughout the rest of the country. The colonists soon surrounded the British in Boston. War had begun.

That June the Second Continental Congress chose Madison's fellow Virginian, George Washington, to organize the revolutionaries gathered around Boston into an army. The conflict was spreading throughout the colonies,

——————————— ✧ ———————————

The Second Continental Congress met in this Philadelphia statehouse. Philadelphia was the main city of the new colonies. It later became the temporary capital, from 1790 to 1800.

including into Virginia. British ships fired cannons on Norfolk, Virginia, on January 1, 1776, setting part of the town on fire. Several months later, Madison and his uncle, William Moore, were chosen to represent their county at a meeting in Williamsburg. The two men spent several days traveling from their home to the colony's capital, braving torrential rains.

The meeting had been called to debate instructions for Virginia's representatives to the Continental Congress. Until this point, the fight against the British had officially been aimed at resisting laws the colonists believed were unfair. Many Americans were not as radical as Madison. They would probably have agreed to remain subjects of the king if some method could have been worked out for self-government and representation in Parliament. But on May 15, the Virginia Convention voted unanimously to tell its representatives to the Continental Congress that America must be a free nation. Madison rejoiced. A few days later, he joined a committee charged with creating a document called a "Declaration of Rights." The declaration included a plan for the future government of Virginia.

One of the clauses in the draft of the declaration referred to religious freedom. Madison considered religion very important and was a firm believer in God. However, he believed religion was a matter between each individual and God. Only a person's own "reason and conviction" could guide his or her devotion, not the force of law or government. Working with George Mason, the head of the committee, Madison proposed a measure stating that "all men are equally entitled to enjoy the free exercise of religion." This measure granted citizens of Virginia the right to practice a variety of religions freely.

JEFFERSON

As the war progressed, Madison continued to serve his country, overseeing local war preparations and helping to organize efforts to support the troops. In 1777 he lost an election to the Virginia legislature (lawmaking body), called the House of Delegates (a delegate is a spokesman). Madison blamed his loss on his refusal to supply liquor to voters on Election Day, a common practice. Later that year, however, the House of Delegates named him to the governor's council. The council assisted the governor and had to review and approve his actions. Madison prepared many of the governor's papers, attending 10 A.M. meetings six days a week in the two-story capitol building.

The first governor Madison worked for was Patrick Henry, a famous and outspoken Patriot (a person who believed the American colonies should be free from Britain). The second, elected in June 1779, was Thomas Jefferson. Jefferson was already famous as the main author of the Declaration of Independence, which had announced America's freedom from Great Britain in 1776. The spark of brilliance in the twenty-eight-year-old Madison excited Jefferson as they worked together in the governor's chambers. The two became fast friends. Both men were freethinkers and shared interests in politics as well as in science and other subjects.

CONGRESS

By 1779 the Revolutionary War was in its fourth year. General Washington was having great difficulty holding his

*Patrick Henry (left) and Thomas Jefferson (right) were both Patriots.
Madison shared similar political views with both men, but he was
especially close to Jefferson.*

army together. One of his biggest problems was the need for
money—both for supplies and to pay his men. Washington
looked to the Continental Congress for help. He complained to his friend George Mason that his home state was
not sending its best people to the Congress. Virginia soon
took the hint. That winter it asked Madison to become one
of the state's representatives in the Continental Congress.
Though at first he resisted, Madison eventually agreed to
travel to Philadelphia, America's new capital.

Madison arrived in Philadelphia in March 1780. He stayed
at the home of Mrs. Mary House, who rented rooms to several members of Congress during the war. Congress met a block
away at the statehouse, later known as Independence Hall.

Many consider Independence Hall the birthplace of America. The Declaration of Independence was signed here in 1776.

✧ ————————————————

Madison soon found himself spending many exhausting and frustrating hours there. The most important and difficult problem was money. There simply wasn't enough of it. And nothing Congress did could change that.

Despite this and other hardships, Washington managed not only to keep his army together but to mount a blistering campaign against the British. Finally, in 1781, he and his troops won a major victory at Yorktown, Virginia. While some fighting continued, the British recognized that they had no hope of winning and began negotiating for peace. Madison remained in Congress during the two years it took after Yorktown for the two countries to agree to a peace treaty. Finally, in 1783, after some eight years of conflict, the United States of America had officially become a free nation.

KITTY

Not all of Madison's efforts in Philadelphia related to his work. Sometime in the winter of 1782–1783, he met and fell in love with a girl named Catherine "Kitty" Floyd. Kitty was fifteen years old that winter, less than half

James Madison's age. The youngest daughter of a New York congressman named William Floyd, Kitty stayed at Mrs. House's with the rest of the Floyd family.

Madison wrote to Jefferson about his interest in Kitty, and Jefferson encouraged him. When Jefferson visited Philadelphia that February, he saw for himself that the two would make a good pair. Marriage to Kitty, he told Madison, would make him "happier than you can possibly be in a single state."

Madison apparently proposed to Kitty in April. According to a letter he sent Jefferson, she accepted, though they decided to delay the announcement until the fall. A few weeks later, Madison rode with the Floyd family as they traveled through New Jersey toward their home. He was planning not just to marry Kitty, but he was going to retire from Congress and go back to his family farm. As a married man, he would have personal responsibilities. He would help run the family business and possibly even expand it or branch out on his own. The future looked bright.

But then, without real explanation, Kitty decided she did not want to marry Madison. Though deeply upset, he took great pains to hide his emotions, even from his friend Jefferson. It would be some time before he loved again.

Young Kitty Floyd broke Madison's heart when she decided not to marry him.

Madison returned home in 1783 after the Revolution.
His political career was just beginning.

CHAPTER THREE

A NEW CONSTITUTION

*"The whole community is big with expectation.
And there can be no doubt but that the result
will in some way or other have a powerful
effect on our destiny."*
—James Madison, telling his friend Thomas
Jefferson in a letter about the start of the
Constitutional Convention

With the war over, Madison left Philadelphia and
returned to Montpelier in December 1783. But it wasn't
long before he turned his attention back to government.
Elected a member of Virginia's legislature in April, he
helped turn back a law that would have prevented slave
owners from freeing slaves. He also worked hard to prevent the kind of money shortage the country had dealt
with during the war.

Not all of his energies were spent on the state government. He helped with the family farm and other business.

He joined George Washington and others in an attempt to develop the rivers of Virginia for travel and trade. That plan, which never came into being, would have required a canal and other improvements, including a newly invented mechanical boat. Madison also studied law and took a trip through northern New York with the Marquis de Lafayette, a famous Frenchman who had fought by Washington's side during the Revolution.

A NEW GOVERNMENT

As he worked as a state legislator, Madison became more and more convinced that the United States needed a strong central government. The country's constitution, known as the Articles of Confederation, did not encourage unity. Worse, the weak constitution made it hard for much to get done on a national level. Under the Articles, each state had an equal representation in a central congress. Nine of the thirteen states had to agree for most proposals to get passed. It was usually difficult, if not impossible, to get agreement.

For many, the problems of a weak government were illustrated in late 1786. That year a farmer named Daniel Shays led other farmers in Massachusetts to revolt against the state government. Economic hard times had led to high debts for farmers in the state. When many couldn't pay their debts, the people they owed money to sued. Afraid that they would lose their land and homes to pay the debts, farmers prevented the courts from meeting and refused to acknowledge their debts. This made the economy even worse and caused confusion and lawlessness.

If the government could not enforce the laws, Madison and others feared, the country would turn to a strong

Daniel Shays led nearly two thousand farmers in the 1786 Shays's Rebellion.

leader—a king—to restore order. The liberty and rights won through the Revolution would be lost.

Still, scrapping the Articles of Confederation was not a popular idea. The states would have to give up much of their own power if a stronger central government was established. The only way to win support for a new constitution was to get important people to back a new plan. And the most important person in the country was General Washington, who had led the army to victory.

Washington agreed that a new government was needed, but he hesitated to get involved. Madison worked to persuade Washington that he was needed. He also started telling others that the retired general agreed a constitutional convention should be held. As a desperate measure, he added Washington's name to a state bill that called for Virginia to send representatives to a constitutional convention.

The bill passed, but Madison had to apologize for going so far against Washington's wishes. "Your name could not be spared," he told Washington as he wrote at his desk in the state capital of Richmond on December 7, 1786. Madison sought each word carefully, not just apologizing but trying to get Washington to change his mind. It was among the most important letters he ever wrote, for without the general's prestige, the plan to write a new constitution would fail.

PROBLEMS WITH GOVERNMENT

While Washington reconsidered attending the constitutional convention, Madison worked hard on a plan to shape the new government. On the one hand, the plan had to provide for a strong central authority that would join all of the states together in a common cause. It had to be strong enough to do difficult and unpopular jobs, such as raising taxes. He also felt that only a strong central government could protect important freedoms, including the freedom of religion.

On the other hand, Madison agreed with those who said that states had to play an important part in the new nation. Local government was critical. After all, it was what the Revolution had been fought over. Madison studied earlier governments around the world, comparing and contrasting them. Finally, he came up with a plan for what he called a "mixed government." This type of government would give important powers to a central government but would still allow the states to retain some power. And the central government would be arranged in such a way that no one person or group would have too much control.

According to Madison's plan, the lawmaking body would be bicameral, or consisting of two parts, or houses. One body of lawmakers would be representatives from each state who were very close to the people. They would be chosen either directly by voters or by state legislatures, which themselves would be chosen directly by the people. Their terms in office would be short. Therefore, these law-makers would reflect the people's immediate wishes. The second body of lawmakers would be elected by members of the first house. Its members' terms would be much longer, so the body would not be subject to rapid change. Madison believed this would remove the second house from everyday problems and politics, allowing these lawmakers to take a long-term view of the country and its needs.

The two bodies working together would balance short-term and long-term answers to problems. Madison also realized the country should have a national executive, or leader, to be in charge of the army and carry out laws passed by the representatives in the two houses. And final-ly, he knew courts would be needed, to make sure that the enforcement of laws was equal and fair.

By the end of March, Washington had decided to join the effort to change the government. On April 16, 1787, Madison wrote him outlining his ideas. "I have sought for some middle ground," he explained, making the argument for his plan. He also shared his ideas with Edmund Randolph, Virginia's governor. Madison, Washington, Randolph, and the four other members of the Virginia del-egation met in Philadelphia in May to prepare for what would become known as the Constitutional Convention. They spent several hours a day talking about Madison's plan, making it better, and discussing it with others. It came to be called the Virginia Plan, and it became the starting point for discussions on the Constitution when the

*Edmund Randolph helped
Madison and the other delegates
draft the U.S. Constitution.*
——————————— ✧

convention finally began at
the end of the month.

THE GREAT COMPROMISE

The delegates had been called
together only to amend, or
revise, the Articles of
Confederation. The Virginia
Plan went far beyond a simple amendment. But Madison's
ideas won acceptance right away. Many details had to be
worked out, but the delegates agreed to use his outline as a
starting point for a brand new Constitution.

After a few weeks, however, they hit a snag. Should
the number of elected representatives from each state be
based on population? Or should every state have the
same number?

While these seemed like simple questions, they were
critical, because they had to do with power. Since Congress
would have the authority to pass laws, the more legislators
a state could send to Congress, the more power it would
have. For example, in 1790 Virginia had about 748,000
people. Under the population plan, Virginia would have
many more representatives (and therefore many more votes
in Congress) than Delaware, which had only about 59,000

citizens. On the other hand, if a small state had the same number of representatives as a large state, then the individual voters of the large state would have much less say in the government. In theory, one person in Delaware would have the power of ten in Virginia.

Under the Virginia Plan, the number of representatives would be based on population. Not surprisingly, delegates from states with small populations objected.

On June 15, delegate William Paterson proposed what came to be known as the New Jersey Plan. (At the time, New Jersey was one of the small states, ranking ninth in population.) Paterson and his supporters suggested a one-house legislature, with each state having the same number of representatives. This was met by a strong attack by New York's

———————————— ✧ ————————————

Delegates debated and crafted the Constitution over four long, hot months.

Alexander Hamilton

——————— ◇ ———————

Alexander Hamilton, a former aide to General Washington and an ally of Madison's. In a six-hour speech on June 18, Hamilton laid the groundwork for a vote the next day. In that vote, a majority of delegates agreed to discard the New Jersey Plan. It was a major victory for Madison's ideas, but the battle between small and large states was not yet resolved.

Debate continued for several days. Madison stuck to his guns. The nation should have two houses of Congress, he argued, and all representatives should be chosen according to population. But as the discussion grew bitter, others saw a need for compromise. Finally, Connecticut delegate Roger Sherman proposed one: why not choose delegates according to population in one house but give each state the same vote in the other house?

Madison opposed the idea, which came to be called the Connecticut Compromise. When a vote was taken among the delegates, all of the smallest states present favored the proposal. All of the larger states opposed it.

The one exception was Massachusetts. The large state's decision in favor of the compromise allowed the measure to triumph. Madison had lost his argument. Yet the compromise helped preserve his ideas about balancing the different needs of the country. These days the house with proportional representation is called the House of Representatives (sometimes referred to as just the House). Each state gets a certain number of representatives based on the population census, which is taken every ten years. In the Senate, each state has two representatives, as they have since the Constitution was adopted.

ARGUMENTS

Madison sat at the front of the room, taking his notes as the debate continued. Many more issues needed to be decided. Washington, who had been chosen the convention president, sat nearby at the front table quietly as he always did, letting the debate proceed without taking part. Summer in Philadelphia was a hot affair, and the arguments were starting to run as hot as the blistering sun. Since the debates were held in secret, without the press or public present, everyone could speak freely. And they did, often arguing bitterly. But the matter at hand was an important one—how should the president be elected?

One of the delegates proposed that the president be selected for fifteen years and chosen by the state governors. Madison set down his pen and asked to speak. He rose, his small frame barely visible from the back of the room. His voice, as usual, was tinny and weak. But his words were strong. The states' governors could not be given the power to choose the president, he declared. Such a scheme would place too much power in the hands of too few people and would be ripe for corruption. The people must elect the president—either directly, or by choosing representatives whose only job was to elect the president.

SLAVERY

The Connecticut Compromise of 1787 included one other important decision that balanced power between the states: how to count slaves. If representation in one house of government was based on population, should slaves be counted? The states that had a lot of slaves wanted them counted. On the other hand, these states insisted that slaves were property, not citizens. They couldn't vote. They had no rights. Most of these states were in the South. States that didn't have many slaves countered that because slaves weren't citizens, they shouldn't be counted at all. These states included most of the North, though slavery was still legal there.

Early in the Constitutional Convention, a compromise was reached to count a slave as three-fifths of a person when basing representation on population. It was an arbitrary number, presented only as a compromise.

Slavery was so controversial, however, that slaves were referred to only indirectly in the finished Constitution. Many of

James Madison

A PLAN

FOR

THE GRADUAL

ABOLITION OF SLAVERY

IN THE

UNITED STATES,

WITHOUT DANGER OR LOSS

TO THE

CITIZENS OF THE SOUTH.

BALTIMORE:
PRINTED BY BENJAMIN LUNDY—CAMDEN STREET.

1825.

—————————— ✧

After the Constitutional Convention, Madison published this pamphlet to convince others that abolishing slavery was a good idea.

the people at the convention wanted to do away with slavery, though they were clearly outnumbered. Madison, whose family owned slaves, was among them.

"Every master of slaves is born a petty tyrant [an unjust ruler]," Madison told the others at the convention. According to biographer Irving Brant, Madison opposed a clause in the Constitution that would specifically allow for a tax on slaves. Madison, wrote Brant, believed "it was wrong . . . to admit in the Constitution that there could be property in men."

If Madison couldn't stop slavery directly, he could slow its spread. "I hold it essential to every point of view that the General Government have power to prevent the increase of slavery," he declared during the debates. But the delegates eventually agreed not to create any laws banning the slave trade as part of a compromise on commerce laws. Madison objected to the proposal but eventually was overruled.

Madison did not like slavery, and his distaste for it would grow through the years. Yet neither he nor anyone else at the convention made a serious effort to ban slavery. He and others knew that southern states would never have agreed to a new constitution if such a measure were included. It would have doomed the Constitution.

The debate over the presidential election grew. Elbridge Gerry of Massachusetts declared that most citizens were too ignorant to elect the president. They would be tricked into choosing bad leaders such as Daniel Shays, whose rebellion in Massachusetts was one of the reasons they were here.

Many agreed. To counter this possibility, Charles Pinckney of South Carolina proposed that only wealthy landowners be allowed to hold office. A representative or judge should have at least $50,000 worth of property or cash, he argued. The president should own property worth $100,000, he suggested.

Madison didn't like that idea. He put the matter to rest with another speech. "If the legislature could . . . [make wealth a requirement for running for office] it can by degrees subvert [overthrow] the Constitution," he declared. "A republic may be converted into an aristocracy [government by the very wealthy] or oligarchy [government by a small, corrupt group] as well by limiting the number capable of being elected, as the number authorized to elect." He had stated an important principle—America must be governed by all, rich and poor.

Again and again, Madison disagreed with others. In general, he fought to preserve the democratic nature of the government. He didn't always win, but as the summer wore on, the Constitution that took shape reflected most of his beliefs. Finally, in September, delegates approved the final draft. It would be presented to the states for a final vote.

Madison said good-bye to the men he'd spent months with and walked back to Mrs. House's. He might have felt relief, but he knew more hard work lay ahead.

CHAPTER FOUR

LION OF THE HOUSE

"The real friends to the Union [the United States] are those who are friends to the authority of the people, the sole foundation on which the Union rests. . . . "

—James Madison, in an article in the *National Gazette* arguing that the people, not the government, must be supreme

The newspaper was about to go to press, and Madison's article wasn't ready. *He must hurry!* He dipped his pen into the ink pot and scrawled feverishly. His thoughts flowed from his head to his paper—and then were snatched up to be set in type.

It was October 1788. Madison was in New York City, helping Hamilton and John Jay, a diplomat and government official, as they tried to convince New Yorkers to support the new Constitution. They were writing a series of essays giving all the reasons for the new form of government. Their articles were written incredibly quickly. Many of them were typeset before the author's ink was dry. Yet they remain some of the most eloquent and important arguments in favor of not just our Constitution but democratic government in general.

These essays are known as the *Federalist Papers*. A total of eighty-five were written, all published under a pen name, or false name, in a number of different newspapers. Each took on a different topic.

Scholars differ on exactly who wrote which essays—Madison and Hamilton's recollections differ. But estimates for Madison range from a low of fourteen to nearly thirty, with most people crediting Madison with twenty-seven or twenty-nine. The essays were originally intended to be published only in New York, where there was great opposition to the new Constitution. But the essays were soon reprinted throughout the country, where they were widely read as American classics.

EARLY VICTORIES

Delaware, New Jersey, Georgia, and Connecticut voted to adopt the Constitution during the early winter of 1787–1788. But

T H E

FEDERALIST:

ADDRESSED TO THE

PEOPLE OF THE STATE OF
NEW-YORK.

NUMBER I.

Introduction.

AFTER an unequivocal experience of the inefficacy of the subsisting federal government, you are called upon to deliberate on a new constitution for the United States of America. The subject speaks its own importance; comprehending in its consequences, nothing less than the existence of the UNION, the safety and welfare of the parts of which it is composed, the fate of an empire, in many respects, the most interesting in the world. It has been frequently remarked, that it seems to have been reserved to the people of this country, by their conduct and example, to decide the important question, whether societies of men are really capable or not, of establishing good government from reflection and choice, or whether they are forever destined to depend, for their political constitutions, on accident and force. If there be any truth in the remark, the crisis, at which we are arrived, may with propriety be regarded as the æra in which

A

that

Madison, Hamilton, and others wrote the Federalist Papers to persuade the states to adopt the Constitution.

debates in the larger states, especially Pennsylvania and Massachusetts, showed that the matter was far from decided. The conflict settled down to two sides. The Federalists supported the Constitution. In general, Federalists included former officers in the revolutionary army as well as businesspeople and others who depended on trade for a living. As a whole, these groups favored a strong central government that could unify the country. Such a government could improve trade conditions by improving transportation and economic conditions. Those against the Constitution, sometimes called "Antis," tended to include farmers and people who favored states' rights over a strong federal government. The debates between the Federalists and the Antis were not only in newspapers. Mobs attacked delegates in Philadelphia when Pennsylvania held a convention to discuss whether to adopt the Constitution.

In Virginia support for the Constitution wavered. Many prominent Virginians were against it. As opposition to the Constitution rose, Madison decided to leave New York in early March. He wanted to be home in time to run for election to the state convention, where adoption of the Constitution would be debated.

As he made his way home, Madison stopped to see an old friend, the Reverend John Leland. The Baptist minister and Madison had worked together in 1784 and 1785 on laws ensuring religious freedom in Virginia. But when Leland opened his door to Madison a week before the election, he told his old friend that he was not supporting the Constitution—or him.

Leland pointed out that the Constitution did not guarantee important rights such as freedom of religion

The Reverend John Leland
———————— ◇ ————————

and freedom of speech. Leland and a growing number of others said they would withhold their support until the rights were guaranteed.

Madison believed strongly in these rights. But he felt it was not necessary to list them in the Constitution. He thought the Constitution should focus on the form of the government. Once it was established, the government itself could pass laws guaranteeing these rights. He also thought that amending (changing) the Constitution at that point would doom it to failure.

Madison soon came up with a compromise. He offered to add the guarantee of rights as amendments to the Constitution after the Constitution was adopted. Leland and others had only Madison's word that he would do this. But his reputation for honesty was so high that they agreed. Madison was elected to the Virginia state convention.

RATIFICATION

Nearly two hundred delegates and aides buzzed with excitement the morning of June 6, 1788, as the Virginians debated the Constitution. The Antis had struck a huge blow the day before, thanks to the powerful lungs of Patrick Henry. The man famous for shouting "Give me liberty, or give me death!" during the Revolution had delivered a speech against the Constitution, claiming that the president would be able to enslave America. No one among the Federalists had half the speaking voice of Henry. Antis began predicting victory.

Madison fiddled with his hat as he waited that morning for his turn to speak. Finally called on, Madison stood, trying to control the nervous energy that made the movement of his arms and legs jerky rather than smooth. A great deal depended on him. Eight states had ratified (passed) the Constitution, but nine were needed. New Hampshire was

——————— ✧ ———————

George Washington (center, standing) *leads a debate among delegates about the Constitution. These debates often lasted for days.*

meeting at this same time, but Madison couldn't be sure how the vote there would go. He wanted to win it here, and to do so, he had to change some minds *immediately*.

He took his notes from his hat and began speaking in his soft voice, his words so low that at times not even the secretary could hear them. He would not use dramatics, he told the audience. Instead, he would debate the Constitution solely on its "merits." Then, one by one, he demolished the claims Henry had made. Madison spoke for the rest of the session and went back at it the next day, patiently but powerfully laying out his case. He was calm, where Henry was loud. He appealed to logic instead of emotion, and he was clearly gaining the upper hand.

But then, suddenly, he stopped speaking. He allowed one of his friends to begin talking. Near collapse, Madison left the hall. He spent the next three days in bed, recovering from exhaustion and what he called a "bilious indisposition." Meanwhile, the debate raged. Madison got out of bed the following week to continue the battle. Physically weak but bursting with mental energy, he guided his team of Federalists. It paid off. On June 25, Virginia adopted the Constitution 88 to 80. It was the tenth state to ratify the Constitution, beaten out by New Hampshire a few days before. James Madison's plan for government had just become the law of the land.

THE PRESIDENT'S MAN

Madison had won the fight for the Constitution in Virginia, but the state legislature was controlled by Patrick Henry and other Antis. They blocked Madison's bid to become a U.S. senator. Instead, urged by friends, he decided to run for the

U.S. House of Representatives. He easily won the election. The Christmas of 1788 found him at George Washington's home, Mount Vernon, celebrating the holiday. Then braving the extreme cold, he headed to New York City, where the new government was just organizing itself. When Congress met in early 1789, among Madison's first actions was to propose a bill establishing high tariffs, or taxes, on luxury imports, such as rum, coffee, and tea, so America could start paying its bills.

As nearly everyone in the country expected, Washington, the hero of the Revolution, was elected president in February 1789. Washington's arrival in New York on April 23 set off a huge celebration in the city and surrounding communities. Washington asked Madison to write his inaugural speech, given to the people as the new president.

Madison was one of Washington's key advisers as well as an important member of Congress. He helped Washington choose his cabinet, a special group of advisers. Each cabinet member, called a secretary, was in charge of a different area. The treasury secretary, for example, was in charge of the

---✧

Washington chose his cabinet carefully. Members included (from left to right) Henry Knox, Thomas Jefferson, Alexander Hamilton, and Edmund Randolph.

government's money. The secretary of state was in charge of diplomatic relations between the United States and other nations. The secretary of war was in charge of the army. The cabinet members had a great deal of power, and choosing them was among Washington's most important early tasks.

Madison was among those recommending Alexander Hamilton for treasury secretary. And he helped the president convince Jefferson to take the job as secretary of state.

Madison also went to work on amendments to the Constitution as he had promised. The amendments were ratified by two-thirds of Congress that September and then sent to the states. They became part of the Constitution in 1791. These first ten amendments to the Constitution, called the Bill of Rights, guarantee freedom of speech, of press, and of religion, as well as the right to bear arms and to have fair trials, among other things.

DEBTS AND RUPTURE

Among the most pressing problems facing the United States were debts left from the Revolution. As secretary of treasury, Hamilton came up with a plan to pay them. At the same time, he wanted to put the U.S. economic system on firm footing. His solution contained several parts.

During the Revolution, soldiers and farmers were paid with certificates promising full payment in the future. In many cases, the people who received these certificates needed money desperately. They had sold their certificates to others at a fraction of the original value.

Hamilton wanted to pay off all of these certificates at their full value. The plan greatly benefited those who had been wealthy enough to buy the certificates at low prices.

Critics said Hamilton favored the rich over patriotic but poor soldiers. Worse, some of Hamilton's friends learned of the plan and bought up the certificates at low prices before others found out. Hamilton also wanted the federal government to take over state debts from the war. Some states, especially those in New England, thought this was a great idea. Others, such as Virginia, had paid off their debts and were angry that other states wouldn't have to do the same.

Madison supported some of Hamilton's plans, but the proposal to pay off the certificates at full value bothered him a great deal. The debate was not just one about money. For Madison, the issue was one of fairness. Many soldiers had been forced to sell off their certificates simply to live. They had done the most work and suffered greatly during the Revolution. They, not those who had bought the certificates, should receive most of the money.

Hamilton argued that it would be impossible to find all of the original owners of the certificates and deal with them fairly. Madison complained bitterly to his father back home when his proposal to aid the "original sufferers" was discarded because of "impracticality."

Madison was also deeply troubled by Hamilton's proposal to take over state debt. And Madison was not ready to give up this fight. He argued that the proposal was unfair to states, such as Virginia, that had worked hard to pay off their debts on their own. To work out a compromise, Hamilton, Jefferson, and Madison met at Jefferson's house on Maiden Lane in New York City. In the end, they agreed on a plan that would allow the federal government to take over state debts. At the same time, they agreed to move the federal capital to the area near the Potomac River, which Madison and other Virginians had wanted for some time.

A NEW FIGHT

Hamilton and Madison had compromised on the question of states' debt, but an even bigger fight loomed. Once again, the men who had worked together to pass the Constitution found themselves at odds. In 1790 Hamilton proposed the Bank Bill, a bill that would allow the government to form a Bank of the United States. This bank, partly owned by the government, would be able to issue money and regulate the economy. In many respects, it was modeled after the highly successful Bank of England.

Madison had several objections. In his opinion, banks were useful and necessary, but they ought to be spread out around the country. Creating one very strong bank, he argued, was a formula for trouble. He thought it would concentrate too much power in one place. But more importantly for Madison, the Constitution did not give the Congress the power to establish banks. He thought the Bank Bill would be a dangerous example. If the government grabbed this power, what would it try next?

The Senate and House voted in favor of the law over Madison's objections. But Madison's opposition troubled Washington. Was Congress acting illegally? How much power did it really have? The two men discussed the matter several times in "free conversations." Washington asked both Jefferson and his attorney general (the government's lawyer), Edmund Randolph, for their opinions. Both declared the law unconstitutional (going against the Constitution).

Hamilton took the opposite view. He argued that creating a bank was necessary to regulate the economy and raise money through taxes. Since the Constitution granted Congress the power to do these things, Hamilton said Congress could go ahead and set up the bank.

Washington weighed all the arguments for several days. Finally, he decided to sign the Bank Bill into law.

AGAINST TOO MUCH POWER

Madison continued to fight against expanding the government's power. And the more he did this, the more he came into conflict with Hamilton and Washington.

On the other hand, he found himself in very close agreement on many issues with Thomas Jefferson. And after the Bank Bill was signed, Jefferson took Madison's advice and offered a State Department job to Madison's old college schoolmate, Philip Freneau. The job was for a clerk to translate newspapers from French into English. But what the two really wanted to do was find a way to support Freneau so he could edit a newspaper. The newspaper would print articles by Madison and others who supported his views. Madison believed a strong voice was needed to counter political articles published in another paper that backed the views of Hamilton, Vice President John Adams, and others. Along with Jefferson and others who shared his views, Madison wanted to push policies favoring farmers and opposing wealthy businessmen.

Freneau's newspaper was called the *National Gazette*. Its first issue came off the press on October 31, 1790—Halloween. It was soon spooking political opponents across the country. Among its most bitter targets was Hamilton.

Rights ahead of His Time

Not all of James Madison's proposals made it into law, not even all of his ideas about the Constitution. Several of his proposed amendments in what became the Bill of Rights, for example, were considered too radical. But they tell us a great deal about what Madison thought. In many cases, Madison was simply ahead of his time.

---------------------------- ✧ ----------------------------

Though not all of his ideas became amendments, Madison played a key role in shaping the Bill of Rights (below).

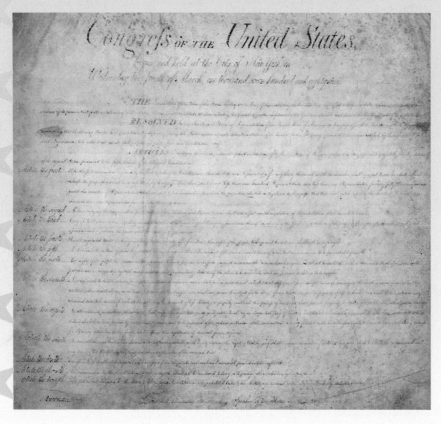

In one amendment, Madison proposed that anyone who had religious objections to "bearing arms," or fighting in a war, could not be forced to do so. These days, our laws provide for release from certain types of military service for conscientious objectors, those who morally object to a war.

In another amendment, Madison proposed that states be forbidden from violating individual rights protected by the Constitution, such as freedom of speech or trial by jury. Madison wanted to ensure that all laws would apply to all citizens equally, wherever they lived. He worried, however, that the states would try to violate some of these rights. As it turned out, they did, especially in the South, where after the Civil War (1861–1865), state laws stripped African Americans of the most basic rights, such as the right to vote. But it was not until the 1950s and 1960s that the federal government finally used its power to uphold individual rights denied by the states during the struggle for equal rights. In those decades, African Americans finally won the long battle for equality. They were assisted by a series of laws, presidential actions, and court orders that showed once and for all that states could not deny rights guaranteed by the Constitution.

Jefferson (right) *and Madison* (left) *had many discussions about how to share their political views with the public.*

STAYING ON

In the spring of 1792, Washington called Madison to his office for an important discussion. The president reminded his friend that when he was first elected he had planned to retire after one four-year term. His term was drawing to a close at the end of the year. Washington intended to carry out his plan and wanted Madison to help write a farewell message.

Madison objected. The country needed Washington, he said. Economic conditions were bad, and people lacked faith in the government. Only Washington could keep up people's hopes.

Washington told Madison he was feeling old and tired. Worse, his two most important cabinet members— Hamilton and Jefferson—were fighting constantly and bitterly over political philosophics. The president saw opposing political groups developing in the country, with each putting its own interests above the common good.

All the more reason to stay, Madison countered. If Washington left, who would succeed him? Not Jefferson, who also wanted to retire. Would it be Vice President Adams? Madison suggested Adams acted too much like a king. Other possibilities were even worse.

Washington insisted. Reluctantly, Madison agreed to write the retirement message. But when he sent it to the president, he added his own note. Washington must not retire, he pleaded. He had to make "one more sacrifice, severe as it may be, to the desires and interests of your country."

Madison wasn't the only one trying to convince him. Others, including Hamilton and Jefferson, had also done so.

——————————— ✧

Vice President John Adams

The president finally gave in, running for and winning reelection even as the fighting in his cabinet continued.

THE SPLIT

At the end of 1793, Jefferson resigned from the cabinet. As a result, Hamilton's influence with Washington seemed to grow. Madison, though still a friend of Washington's, found himself opposed to many of the president's policies. For one, he did not agree with the president's neutral stance toward Great Britain. Madison was outraged by British policies against America, which included seizing American

————————————— ◆ —————————————

George Washington (center, in black coat) *at his second inauguration, held in Philadelphia. Many people celebrated, just as they had done four years earlier.*

ships in the West Indies. He pushed for more support of the French in their latest conflict with Great Britain, even though the president wanted to remain neutral. Madison also fought against taxes proposed by Hamilton and supported by Washington. He felt the taxes unfairly singled out the South.

American politicians gradually split into two camps, which soon became political parties. One camp was known as the Federalists. Adams and Hamilton were among the most prominent leaders. Jefferson, Madison, and others were known as Republicans and Democratic-Republicans (later known as Democrats). The word *Federalist*, which once had described Madison very accurately, came to be a curse on his lips.

By 1794 James Madison was a leader in Congress and one of the most important men in America. He was also still a bachelor at forty-three. He seemed destined to live out the rest of his life consumed totally by politics, without a wife or children. Or was he?

CHAPTER FIVE

LOVE AND HATE

"[You] must come to me. Aaron Burr says that the great little Madison has asked to be brought to see me this evening."

—Dolley Payne Todd, writing to her friend on the day of her first meeting with James Madison

She was the most beautiful woman in the largest city in America. And James Madison, the author of some of the most important speeches in the country's history, stood tongue-tied before her.

Madison might be a famous congressman, but he felt like a giddy schoolboy when he met Dolley Payne Todd on a spring evening in 1794. Exactly Madison's height, Dolley was not quite twenty-five. A lovely widow with a young son, her eyes and lively manner instantly captured and enchanted all who saw her. The evening Aaron Burr introduced them, her red dress seemed to set the room on fire. It certainly ignited Madison's heart.

When Madison met the lovely Dolley Payne Todd in 1794, he was instantly charmed by her.

——————————— ✧

DOLLEY

Dolley was born June 20, 1768, to John and Mary Coles Payne near present-day Guilford College in North Carolina. The family counted a number of important Virginia relatives, including Patrick Henry, whose mother and Dolley's maternal grandmother were sisters. As followers of the Quaker religion, Dolley's parents refused to take oaths of allegiance to any earthly power. They would not support wars, enlist in the army, or pay taxes to support the Revolution. These things made them unpopular with their neighbors, which may have been a factor in the family's decision to move to Philadelphia in 1783. Quakers had originally settled Philadelphia, and many Quakers were among the city's thirty thousand inhabitants.

When she was twenty-one, Dolley married John Todd, a twenty-six-year-old lawyer. John did well as a lawyer, and Dolley soon gave birth to a son, John Payne Todd, on February 29, 1792. Pregnant again the following year,

Dolley gave birth to a baby boy in August 1793. When the boy was still an infant, a terrible epidemic (widespread disease) of yellow fever hit the city. John brought Dolley and the boys to Gray's Ferry in the countryside, which was thought to be healthier. Then he returned to his duty as a Quaker, helping the sick in Philadelphia.

Hundreds of people died in the epidemic. In early October, John Todd's father and mother passed away. John, too, came down with the disease but managed to struggle to Gray's Ferry, where he died in Dolley's arms. Dolley and her infant son also became sick, though historians are not

—————————————— ✦ ——————————————

Dolley and John Todd lived in this grand brick house in Philadelphia, on the corner of Fourth and Walnut streets.

positive that it was from yellow fever. The infant died. With a two-year-old toddler to raise and a heavy heart, Dolley returned to the city.

ROMANCE AND MARRIAGE

When Madison met Dolley in the spring of 1794, it was love at first sight. An acquaintance told Dolley that "he thinks so much of you in the day that he has lost his tongue." By June, James had asked Dolley to marry him, but she hesitated. Nearly twenty years separated them in age. She had a small son and had only recently lost her husband. They were also from different religions, although Madison's record of fighting for freedom of religion must have impressed her. At first, Dolley put him off. But Madison worked hard to win her over. By the time he left for Virginia that June, she seemed to be leaning toward saying yes.

Then disaster struck. Dolley went to visit relatives in Hanover County, Virginia. There she became deathly ill, possibly from malaria. Madison, meanwhile, had to care for a sick Frenchman at his family home. He was the only one there who could speak the sick man's language. When word came of Dolley's illness, he feared he would lose her forever. He was torn between his duty to a sick friend and the love of his life. Finally, a letter arrived saying Dolley was getting better.

"I cannot express, but hope you will conceive the joy it gave me," he wrote back. His words were stilted and formal as he spoke of his love for Dolley, but his emotion was plain. He wanted her to be his wife and never again to be separated. Dolley agreed finally, and on September 15,

1794, she and the man she called "the great little Madison" were wed. "In this union I have everything that is soothing and grateful," Dolley wrote to a friend. "And my little Payne will have a generous protector."

Marriage changed Madison's life in many ways. Biographers have described it as a true partnership, noting that Dolley's admiration deepened into true love as the years went on. There was never any doubt of love on Madison's side. He thought highly of his wife and depended on her for emotional support constantly.

Marriage brought Madison great joy, but it also made him think differently about money. His salary as a congressman was not very large. He had bought land on his own in New York's Mohawk Valley and with his brother on the Virginia frontier as investments. But his finances really depended on the family farm, which his father still ran with the help of his brother Ambrose. As the oldest brother, Madison knew he would inherit it one day. Still, he must have started to think about leaving Congress so he could improve the family income.

REBELLION

In the summer of 1794, opposition to the Whiskey Tax caused a small band of farmers in western Pennsylvania to revolt. The tax, suggested by Hamilton, had been passed by Congress in 1791 to help pay the national debt. The farmers refused to pay the tax and threatened all who tried to collect it. President Washington himself called out the militia and rode to the area to restore order.

The rebellion quickly died out, but in the meantime, many local groups denounced the tax and the government

Many tax collectors who tried to impose the Whiskey Tax were tarred and feathered by angry farmers.

that imposed it. The groups were known as Democratic Societies and, for the most part, sided with Republican congressmen. Members of some of these same groups had helped put down the rebellion. Still, Washington criticized them and the Republicans in Congress for stirring up feelings against the government. He seemed to be saying that people shouldn't criticize the government. The Republicans attacked him for being antidemocratic.

Madison had not supported the rebellion and saw its prompt collapse as a good thing. But Washington's criticism stung. He called it the "greatest error of [Washington's] political life." Madison felt torn between his friendship and admiration for Washington and his dearly held principle of freedom of speech. Madison also felt that the government's power must be held in check. These beliefs proved stronger than friendship. His relationship with Washington went steadily downhill, though he continued to respect the president.

When Washington presented a treaty with Great Britain (known as the Jay Treaty) for ratification in the winter of 1795, the political split became wider and more bitter. For a variety of reasons, Republicans tended to favor France over Great Britain, while Federalists favored Great Britain. The terms of the treaty greatly favored Britain, and even Washington had doubts about it. The treaty was ratified by the Senate, but the House of Representatives still had to vote on a bill to fund some of its measures.

When debate began the following year, Madison claimed that the House had the right to consider and examine the treaty itself, a right not stated in the Constitution. Leading the fight against the treaty, he gained several allies, including Albert Gallatin of Pennsylvania. Madison convinced a majority of the House to ask Washington to turn over papers relating to the Jay Treaty. These papers would include instructions and other material used during treaty negotiations. While the

————————✧

Madison found a close ally and new friend in fellow Republican Albert Gallatin.

fight was over the treaty, two important constitutional issues were involved in asking for the papers.

The first issue was the right of the House of Representatives to act on foreign treaties, which was granted only to the Senate by the Constitution. The second was the independence and role of the president. Some people argued that if the House of Representatives could order the president to turn over his papers, it could tell him to do nearly anything. The executive branch would not be an equal branch of government. It would be working for Congress.

Madison gave two long speeches to the House. In them, he argued that the representatives would not be going against the Constitution if they reviewed treaties when debating whether to fund them. In order to make a proper decision, he argued, the House was entitled to all important materials, including the president's own letters.

Washington refused Madison's request to view the papers relating to the treaty. The executive branch must remain independent from Congress, he argued. And the House of Representatives could not take powers it was not supposed to have.

Talk of war with Great Britain if the treaty wasn't passed and economic considerations cost Madison allies. Even though Washington didn't budge, funding for the Jay Treaty was agreed to by a 51 to 48 vote, with Madison on the losing side.

A NEW PRESIDENT

Tired from eight long years of governing the country and worn out by the political bickering, Washington went ahead with his plan to retire at the end of his second term. He took the letter Madison had written for him in 1792 and gave it to Hamilton to update. Then he had it printed in the newspapers so there would be no chance of his being talked out of retirement a second time.

The election presented the Republicans, who were still more of a loose association than a formal party, with a chance at the presidency. Madison wanted Jefferson to run. Jefferson told him no. But Madison and many others continued to back the retired secretary of state anyway. In those days, there was no formal campaigning, and it was possible for a reluctant candidate to do much better than he wanted. One of Jefferson's leading biographers, Dumas Malone, says that Jefferson "silently acquiesced," or agreed, to the candidacy, though he kept saying he did not want the job. The Federalists backed Vice President John Adams.

In those days, the presidential electors (the men in each state chosen to represent the voters during presidential elections) were picked in different ways decided by each state's legislature. The results took a while to compile. On December 19, 1796, Madison wrote to Jefferson that "the returns from N. Hampshire, Vermont, South Carolina and Georgia, are still to come" but that it looked as if Jefferson would finish second in the balloting. That would make him vice president. Madison worried that Jefferson would refuse the position and urged him not to "withdraw yourself."

Jefferson soon learned the tally: 71 for John Adams, 68 for himself. He sent Madison a letter to pass on to Adams congratulating the new president. The letter was full of such enthusiasm that Madison didn't give it to Adams. Madison told Jefferson that he was worried Adams might misinterpret the letter. He might think that it meant Jefferson, as vice president, would always support him no matter what he did. Madison was playing the role of watchful politician, careful about the ways things might be interpreted by others, worried about the future.

EXPERIMENTAL FARMER

Madison might have wanted Jefferson back in office, but Madison had already decided to leave Congress himself after the 1796 session. His father was very sickly. The family farm and related businesses needed Madison's supervision. He also probably was tired of the political fighting and wanted to have more time off to spend with his wife and stepson.

Madison sold his property in the Mohawk Valley and used the money to expand and remodel the house at Montpelier. Dolley's sister, Anna Payne, came to live with

—————————————— ◇ —— ——————————————

Montpelier was a grand house that sat at the center of the Madison plantation. The Madisons enjoyed entertaining friends and relatives there.

them. His parents and sister Fanny also lived there. Madison supervised the construction of a flour mill and began a system of crop rotation and other scientific methods at the farm. He oversaw the farm and the estate of his brother Ambrose, who had died in 1793. Life for the Madisons settled into a series of pleasant duties and entertainment. They gave parties and visited with a circle of friends and relatives who lived in the area.

FOREIGN TENSIONS AND THE ALIEN AND SEDITION ACTS

America's relations with France had declined while Washington was president. By the time Adams took over, French privateers were capturing American ships and taking their cargo. Privateers were ships captained by private citizens. These ships were granted permission by their government to attack foreign ships. This practice could be quite profitable, since the privateers would keep the goods they captured.

Adams sent diplomats to France to work out disagreements. But the French minister had three of his agents demand a bribe of $250,000 before agreeing to meet with them. The American diplomats refused. Relations got worse, and a war with France seemed likely.

Many Republicans, remembering France's help during the Revolution, were still friendly toward the nation. They wanted to know why the negotiations had failed. Thinking Adams was at fault, they pressed him for the papers relating to the diplomatic mission. Adams finally gave them to Congress, but he crossed out names of the French agents who had demanded the bribe and substituted "X," "Y," and "Z." The effect of this so-called

This political cartoon refers to the XYZ Affair and shows American diplomats refusing to give bribe money to a greedy French monster.

XYZ Affair on the public was the opposite of what Republicans wanted: the public was outraged at France's scandalous behavior and called for war.

In 1798 the Federalists passed four bills that together became known as the Alien and Sedition Acts. The laws made it harder for immigrants to become citizens and allowed the president to deport (send back) as "aliens" any immigrant he considered dangerous. They also gave the president the right to imprison enemy aliens for no crime during wartime and threatened newspaper publishers who criticized the government with fines and jail.

Many immigrants were considered supporters of the Republican Party. And the limits on the press were directly aimed at Adams's Republican critics. But these laws also struck at the heart of the American democracy. They went against the Bill of Rights, which guaranteed a fair trial as well as freedom of speech and press.

Jefferson kept Madison informed of developments as Republicans were criticized, harassed, and threatened with jail. Madison fumed. If a president could jail someone for criticizing him, how could a fair election ever be held? It would be impossible to make even the simplest campaign speech, since backing a candidate different from the president's choice was the same as criticizing the president.

The laws were actually used very few times, but just the threat was enough to clamp down on freedom of speech. Jefferson tried to organize opposition to the measures, even though they were very popular. Finally, Kentucky adopted resolutions written by Jefferson denouncing the laws on November 16, 1798.

Madison prepared a similar protest for Virginia. But he and Jefferson disagreed on one important matter. Jefferson thought that the Alien and Sedition Acts were illegal and unconstitutional. Madison did not agree with his claim that the states could take away the authority they had granted to the national government. This argument would mean that the states were more important than Congress. It also meant that they could secede, or break off, from the Union. Madison remained convinced that the country must stay together. It needed a strong central authority, even if that authority tried to overstep its bounds.

After much urging by Republicans, Madison ran for election to the state legislature in 1799. Following his election, he continued to work against the restrictive Alien and Sedition Acts. But protest was not popular.

At the same time, tensions with France continued to be heated, and many people called for war against the European nation. Adams declined to ask Congress to declare war, but he did direct American ships and privateers to battle the French navy in an unofficial war. Finally, in 1799 Adams was able to start negotiations with France, which led to a peace between the two nations. A year later, three of the restrictive laws were allowed to expire in 1800.

ELECTION OF 1800

President Adams's popularity suffered after he found it necessary to impose direct taxes on property. At the same time, he split with Hamilton and others in the party over several issues, which weakened his position. As the presidential election of 1800 approached, Madison realized that the Republicans would have a good chance against Adams. Once again, Madison and other Republicans backed Jefferson, with Aaron Burr as the vice presidential candidate.

Madison wrote letters to fellow Republicans across the country, helping to coordinate the fight. The new political party had one key strategy—stick together. The Republican presidential electors must vote for both of their candidates, Jefferson and Burr. The strategy seems simple, but at the time, it was unusual. Electors would cast two votes, usually naming the other party's presidential candidate for vice president. This sort of split had enabled Jefferson to become vice president in the last election.

The new strategy worked, but too well. Jefferson and Burr received the same number of votes. Even though party members intended that Burr be the vice president, there was no way of indicating this on the ballots. Burr would not withdraw, even though he claimed he was still loyal to Jefferson. Madison believed that Burr was plotting to become president on his own.

The tie had to be presented to the House of Representatives for a decision, as the Constitution directed. And since the Federalists controlled the House, the Republicans' bitter enemies would decide who the next president would be.

CHAPTER SIX

SECRETARY OF STATE

*"Let us, then, with courage and confidence
pursue our own Federal and Republican
principles, our attachment to union and
representative government."*
—Thomas Jefferson, pleading for unity in his first
inaugural address, 1801

Rumors of plots and possible revolts were everywhere in
Washington, D.C. Pennsylvania's governor got twenty thousand guns ready for the state militia in case the Federalists
refused to name a Republican president. People whispered
about deals that might be made. Some wondered if, instead
of hosting its first inauguration, the new capital city would
see the collapse of the American government.

The Federalists hated Jefferson with a passion. They
didn't want to see him become president, but how far
would they go? Would they vote in his vice president as
president, turning the Republican Party upside down?

Would they select another person entirely, ignoring their duty under the Constitution to pick between the top two candidates? Would they simply not make a selection at all and throw everything into deeper chaos?

Madison heard all of the rumors and worked his hardest to bolster support for his friend Jefferson. But he worked under a great hardship—he was too sick to leave home. Rheumatism, a painful disease that inflamed his joints, made it difficult for him to get out of bed, much less travel. He wrote letters, some extremely angry, urging support and offering advice.

The Federalists were split on what to do, which increased the rumors and confusion. Hamilton urged his fellow party members to vote for Jefferson over Burr. Hamilton greatly disliked Jefferson, but thought he would make a better president than Burr. Hamilton felt Burr could not be trusted. But other influential Federalists detested Jefferson and would probably have voted for the devil before him.

Finally, Congress began meeting in state delegations as directed by the Constitution to select between Burr and Jefferson. Each delegation, or collection of state representatives, had one vote for the presidency. A total of nine out of sixteen votes were needed to select the president. The debate raged from late December 1800 to February 1801, when voting began. At first, Jefferson did not have the necessary votes to win. But eventually, enough Federalists gave in, and Jefferson was named the new president.

A NEW START

At his inauguration in March, Jefferson tried to reach out to everyone. "We are all republicans—we are all federalists," he said.

*Despite Federalist opposition, Jefferson became
the third president of the United States.*

——————— ✧ ———————

Madison was unable to attend the ceremony in Washington. His health was still poor, and his father had just died. While grieving, he had to settle his father's estate, making sure that those named in the will received a fair share of their inheritance. The family business and property holdings were so complicated that the Madisons had to let a court decide on a fair plan to split things up. In the end, James received the house and, after all of the arrangements were finished, three farms totaling 5,000 acres.

In the meantime, Jefferson appointed Madison secretary of state. Along with Albert Gallatin, who became the treasury secretary, Madison was the most influential member of the new president's cabinet. While the Federalists made fun of Madison's short height, they could not challenge his advice or intellect. He tended to be modest and soft-spoken, but his words counted a great deal, whether voiced to the president or to other government or party leaders.

THE LOUISIANA PURCHASE

As secretary of state, Madison was responsible for international relations. He had never been outside of America because of his weak health, and he couldn't travel abroad. But he sent envoys, or representatives, and used letters to communicate with them. His overall goals were to help the United States expand and earn a place as an important country. His biggest problems were with France and Great Britain, the two superpowers of the day.

Since the Revolution, Americans had sought free navigation down the Mississippi River. In the days before railroads, highways, and airplanes, rivers were an all-important means of travel. One obstruction to free trade on the river was Spain, which controlled New Orleans at the mouth of the river. In the fall of 1802, the Spanish closed the city to U.S. goods and forbade all non-Spanish ships from stopping there. This violated a treaty signed in 1795. Secretary of State Madison immediately began working to have the port reopened. But he also recognized a greater problem north of the city, where the French controlled and occupied Louisiana. One of his envoys to France, Robert Livingston, was trying to get the French to sell part of the Louisiana Territory (an area of the United States stretching from the Mississippi River to the Rocky Mountains)—an attempt that included hints of bribes. Nothing came of these moves, and by January 1803, it seemed as if U.S. and French troops in the Mississippi area might go to war over territory and trading rights. Jefferson and Madison sent a new envoy, fellow Virginian James Monroe, to soothe talk of war.

Madison provided a series of instructions covering everything that might happen or be suggested. He also wrote up sample treaties for Monroe to use. The negotiations, Madison insisted, must make New Orleans part of the United States. Spain had just given the city to the French, which at least made it possible to address the problems together. Madison wanted to protect trade on the Mississippi. He also hoped to encourage future expansion and growth in the West.

Before negotiations could begin, France's ruler, Napoleon Bonaparte, decided to sell all of the Louisiana Territory to the United States. Madison was all in favor of the proposal,

and so was the president. A price of $15 million was eventually negotiated. Interest on the payments would nearly double the final price, but history would judge the cost a bargain.

Relations with Great Britain were even more complicated, especially after Great Britain and France went to war in May

✧ ─────────────

James Monroe (left) was sent to replace Robert Livingston as envoy to France in 1803.

Napoleon sold the Louisiana Territory to the United States in 1803 to help pay off his country's debts.

————————— ✧

1803. The British blockaded French ports in France and much of the rest of Europe where Napoleon had seized control. The British proclaimed the right to seize U.S. ships bound for French harbors. Just as troubling was the British policy of boarding American ships and taking sailors they claimed were British deserters, even if the sailors had papers identifying them as American citizens. The policy was called impressment, and it was one of the most emotional disagreements between the two countries.

Monroe was once more sent as a special delegate, this time to Great Britain to work on the disagreements. He negotiated a treaty, but it failed to bring an agreement to end impressment or restore free trade. Jefferson and Madison decided not to submit the treaty to the Senate for ratification, since they believed it would fail.

LIFE IN WASHINGTON

While her husband tended to foreign affairs, Dolley arranged their active social life. Jefferson's wife had died before he became president, and Dolley often acted as a hostess at the President's House. (It was not yet known as the White House.) She welcomed visitors and put them at ease during Jefferson's many informal gatherings. Madison, too, could be a lively host. He was often joking, sometimes telling "ludicrous" or silly stories for the entertainment of all.

Madison usually wore a black suit with a simple white handkerchief. Dolley's wardrobe on formal occasions could be quite fancy and colorful, but otherwise she dressed plainly, as her upbringing as a Quaker had taught her to do. Her only jewelry was her engagement ring, which had rose-shaped diamonds. Madison had begun to bald and would comb his hair forward over the spot. Dolley

─────────── ✧ ───────────

For their time period, James and Dolley Madison dressed very simply.

powdered his hair each day, tying it in a style that had been popular before and during the Revolution but had become a little dated. The couple were very close, and many people commented on how attached they were. They seem to have been unable, however, to have a child of their own, though they raised John Payne Todd together.

Washington was still a very young city, with more open space than buildings. The Madisons lived in a large house on F Street. They often hosted parties there. After dinner, guests might enjoy a game of backgammon as well as conversation. Madison was also fond of chess. He studied moves very carefully, considering each step before proceeding. This habit often carried over into his dealings as secretary of state. He tended to consider his actions very carefully, covering every possible outcome before deciding to proceed.

THE EMBARGO ACT

Great Britain and France remained at war. The United States continued to be caught in the middle. As the conflict continued, the two European nations both seized foreign ships trading with the enemy. In effect, France and Britain demanded that other countries choose sides in the war. Neutral commerce, or trading, with both sides would not be possible. The situation with Britain became even worse when a British ship attacked and then boarded a U.S. warship named *Chesapeake*. The attack occurred off the American coast in 1807. Madison met with a British diplomat over the incident. But he was unable to reach an agreement to end impressment or other undesirable British policies.

Before and during the Revolution, Americans had tried to pressure Britain by stopping trade. They believed that this caused economic hardship in Great Britain and led the British to change their policies. While modern historians say the measures failed, U.S. leaders at the time thought they worked and had a great deal of faith in such laws. After the *Chesapeake* incident, Jefferson backed a new proposal by Gallatin to ban all exports (goods sold to other countries). The law also limited goods bought from Great Britain. His goal was to pressure Great Britain and France to restore the right of countries to remain neutral and continue selling items to whomever they wanted.

In theory the law would apply to all countries equally. But Great Britain remained the largest target, since it had a great deal of trade with the United States. Madison strongly supported the measure, believing it would end British actions against the United States and avoid war. Congress passed the Embargo Act on December 22, 1808.

But the measure hurt Americans more than anyone had foreseen. Farmers suffered greatly because they could no longer sell their goods overseas. The country went into a recession (a period of reduced economic activity). Meanwhile, smugglers took goods to and from Canada, over the Great Lakes, and through Florida. Neither Great Britain nor France changed its policies. As tempers flared, the United States moved closer to war with both countries.

In the meantime, the country got ready for another presidential election. As Jefferson neared the end of his second term, others in the capital expected Madison to run for president. Madison surprised no one, therefore, when he told friends in the winter of 1807 that he would run. In 1808 he won in the electoral votes against Charles Pinckney, the Federalist candidate. George Clinton, vice president under Jefferson, became Madison's vice president as well.

As Madison prepared his inaugural address, he worried about what to do about the conflict between Great Britain and France. Great Britain's actions against U.S. shipping had led to calls of war in the United States. Madison knew he had to stand up for his country's rights, or the nation would be nothing more than a British colony again. But he was worried that his country, which lacked an army and navy, was ill-prepared for war.

CHAPTER SEVEN

WAR ON THE HORIZON

"In reviewing the conduct of Great Britain
toward the United States our attention
is . . . drawn to . . . warfare which is known
to spare neither age nor sex. . . . "
—James Madison, asking Congress to
declare war on Great Britain

The winter lifted early in Washington, D.C., during the year 1809. When Madison rode in his carriage down Pennsylvania Avenue toward the Capitol, a crowd of several thousand people cheered him on in the spring weather. The new president walked into the building with a sense of urgency, preparing to give his inaugural speech. He seemed pale, weighed down by the problems facing America. He even trembled as he approached the podium. But as he started to speak, Madison gradually grew more at ease. He gave a short speech which denounced war as "bloody and wasteful" and went on to say that he cherished peace. Even so, he mentioned in his speech that "an armed and trained militia is the firmest bulwark [defense] of republics."

It was a short but important sentence. Until then, most Republicans, including Madison, had been opposed to having large armies and navies during peacetime. They were afraid that the government might use the armed forces to oppress the people. In the event of war, they argued, there would be ample time to organize an effective army and navy.

Madison came to see that this line of reasoning was wrong. Not having a strong army and navy made it difficult to stand up to countries that had them. And if the other countries declared war, there would be no time to waste.

Madison had concluded that war was likely. He had to expand and organize the military and order new ships built before the war came. But he made no mention of his plans in the ten-minute inaugural speech, and he didn't talk about them later when his guests filled the house on F Street for a celebration. Dolley, as beautiful as ever, wore a pearl necklace in honor of the occasion. The French minister and the British minister met the Madisons at the inaugural ball at Long's Hotel that evening. One escorted Dolley, the other her sister. The new president seemed worn out by the celebration and soon left for home.

Dolley and James Madison held many receptions and parties at the president's mansion in the weeks and years that followed. Ice cream, which had been brought over from France by Jefferson, was a favorite dessert. Dolley was a wonderful host, and the president's sense of humor shone through his cares. While he remained shy in crowds, Madison was lively in small groups and at ease with his friends and relatives. The Madisons spent several months a year at

The President's House was the setting for many gala events while Madison was in office. Dolley loved entertaining politicians, friends, and relatives there.

Montpelier. These vacations were restful for the president and helped restore his health, which was stressed by his job.

NO MORE EMBARGO

Three days before Madison became president, Congress had repealed the unpopular Embargo Act. In its place, Congress passed the Nonintercourse Act. This law banned all trade with Great Britain and France, as well as their colonies, but allowed trade with the rest of the world. While the difference seems minor, the act was easier to get around than the Embargo Act. British goods might be purchased from a neutral country—or receipts might claim that such was the case. A U.S. ship might sail to a neutral port, where the goods it contained might be unloaded and then sent on to France.

The new law was a way for the government to get rid of the old law without admitting that it hadn't worked.

For a few months after Madison's election, Great Britain seemed to make an effort at peace. A new minister, David M. Erskine, worked with Madison on a new treaty agreeing to American conditions. Madison promised to suspend the Nonintercourse Act. But in July, the British government said Erskine had agreed to things he wasn't authorized to negotiate. Once more the British clamped down, impressing seamen and seizing U.S. ships. Napoleon, meanwhile, also ordered that U.S. ships be seized at sea. The United States was being pushed hard by both sides.

Even so, Madison failed to get Congress to prepare for war. A measure to build new ships was defeated in a close vote, 62 to 59 in the House, with some Republicans joining the Federalists to defeat it. Congressmen shouted

———————————— ✧ ————————————

This drawing depicts British soldiers taking control of a U.S. ship.

for war and then failed to find the money to pay for it. Part of the problem was Madison's own doing. He and other Republicans had preached against large government spending and had argued against having a large military. It was difficult to change the minds of many Republicans who had shared those views. Some historians criticize Madison for not being forceful enough when trying to get funding.

RELIGIOUS FREEDOM

Madison remained vigilant on issues regarding religious freedom. In early 1811, Congress passed a bill that created an Episcopal church in the District of Columbia. The law set out how the church's minister and governing board would be named and also gave the church authority to help the poor and educate children.

While well intended, Madison realized the law violated the First Amendment, which guaranteed religious freedom by forbidding the government from making laws about churches or religion. Worse, others might use it as an example to pass other laws about religion. While a law might start out as well meaning, it could one day be used to tell people how they should worship God. Government must never do that, said Madison. He vetoed, or overturned, the bill. Once more, Madison had acted to preserve religious freedom.

WAR

As Madison's first term in office came to a close, Britain and France continued to capture U.S. ships, take U.S. goods without payment, and impress U.S. citizens as virtual slaves aboard ships. At the same time, the British had been encouraging Native Americans who lived in the West to launch attacks against the Americans. Americans felt as though they were being pushed around by the superpowers. Many thought the only way this would stop was by striking back, in other words, going to war.

Madison agreed. His private secretary, Edward Coles, said the president was "reluctant" to go to war but, in the end, felt he had no choice. But Madison decided he could not go to war with both Great Britain and France at the same time. He told Jefferson in a letter that this would create a "thousand difficulties." Madison decided to accept a fresh French promise to stop its attacks, even though he probably didn't believe it. On June 1, 1812, he asked Congress to declare war against Great Britain, while reserving the right to do so against France in the future.

Congress declared war on June 18, starting what became known as the War of 1812. But then Congress declined to increase funding for the navy as Madison asked. Problems multiplied. The army couldn't recruit as many soldiers as it needed. Nonetheless, Madison authorized an invasion of Canada, which was British territory. The idea made sense, since the British had few troops there. A strong attack might end their support of the Native Americans in the West and lead to negotiations for peace.

There were problems from the start. The Massachusetts and Connecticut governors—both Federalists—refused to call out their states' militias to help. Disorganization in Madison's War Department made things even worse. The incompetence of a U.S. general leading the effort, William

William Hull's poor leadership caused the Americans to lose their first battle in the War of 1812. ✧

Hull, doomed the attack. In the end, the U.S. force suffered a humiliating defeat that left the West nearly defenseless. Two thousand Americans were taken prisoner.

Madison did not direct the army personally, but he was responsible for choosing the men who led it, especially the secretary of war, John Armstrong. Armstrong was a poor leader. He quarreled with the other members of Madison's cabinet and undermined the president's authority and power. Madison told him to prepare defenses around Washington, D.C. Armstrong neglected to do so. Yet Madison refused to fire him. The president wanted to "preserve harmony and avoid changes" in his administration. This might have worked well when he was in Congress, where it was important to get different people to agree. But it was a disaster for a president in wartime. It meant poor leaders stayed in command.

Things went from bad to worse. In Europe the British finally had France's Napoleon on the run. That allowed Britain to send more ships to fight against the United States. The British forces were ordered not only to seize U.S. ships but to bomb U.S. towns on the coast.

With the attacks growing and opposition to Madison
increasing, he barely won reelection in 1812. His opponent
was DeWitt Clinton of New York, who was a cousin of
George Clinton. Although he was a Republican, DeWitt
Clinton opposed the war, and the Federalists joined with
him as their candidate to oppose Madison. But Madison
won victories in Pennsylvania, along with most of the
South and the new state of Ohio to win.

In February 1813, a group of British ships under
Admiral Sir John Warren blocked off New York Harbor and
every port to the south. Even as Madison was sworn in as
president a second time, the nearby waters were not safe for

——————————— ✧ ———————————

*Madison ordered an attack against the British after they blockaded
New York Harbor. This British cartoon criticizes the United States's
use of torpedoes and other explosives during that attack.*

U.S. ships. "Fears and alarms" circulated in Washington, Dolley wrote a friend. There were rumors that the Potomac River would be invaded.

Madison authorized a new attack in the North near the Great Lakes. Shipwrights went to work building vessels to dominate Lake Erie and help prevent the invasion. The ships, under the command of Admiral Oliver Hazard Perry, defeated the British, who had to retreat to Canada from Detroit. General William Henry Harrison then defeated a large British and Indian force, securing the West from attack.

But the British had no intention of giving up.

CHAPTER EIGHT

TRIUMPH AT LAST

"When the battle had decidedly commenced, I observed to the Secretary of War and Secretary of State that it would be proper to withdraw to a position in the rear, where we could act according to circumstances. . . ."

—James Madison, recounting the battle near Washington, D.C., in 1814. He had been on the front lines when the British advance began.

The dispatch that Madison had dreaded for months arrived on the morning of August 18, 1814. He read it immediately and flew into action. Four thousand British troops had landed thirty-five miles southeast of Washington. Supported by fifty ships, they were marching north.

The secretary of war scoffed. Armstrong had resisted Madison's directions to build up defenses around the city since the beginning of the war. This time, he claimed the British were aiming at Baltimore, Maryland, well to the north, and would leave Washington alone. Madison himself ordered defenses prepared. U.S. troops moved into the area. Monroe, serving as Madison's secretary of state, took off on a horse to scout the British army.

The British, though they met no resistance, moved very slowly. After four days, they were still fifteen miles from the nation's capital. In the meantime, Madison ordered the national records taken away for safekeeping. He also suggested that Dolley leave the city. But she refused. She told him she wasn't afraid. She also pledged to personally make sure that important presidential papers were not lost.

As the British approached, the president rode to the U.S. lines outside of Washington, D.C., where U.S. troops were preparing to meet the British attack. The next day, he personally questioned two British deserters and found out that their army was definitely going to attack Washington.

"Be ready at a moment's warning," he told his wife, urging her to prepare to escape.

The British attack began on August 24. The U.S. forces outnumbered the British about two to one. But the Americans were so badly organized that the British were able to push them back easily. Twenty-six Americans died, and another fifty-one were wounded. British deaths were higher—sixty-four killed, two hundred fifty wounded. But by four o'clock in the afternoon, they had an open path to the city.

Madison, meanwhile, rushed back to the President's House. Dinner waited for him on the table. Dolley had left it before hurrying out of town in a wagon with the president's papers, some valuable silver, and a portrait of George Washington. Their clothes and much else remained in the house. He left barely ahead of the first British troops.

The British set Washington on fire that night. The president's mansion, the Capitol Building, and many other buildings were burned. Only a severe storm prevented more destruction. The British left Washington on August 25 and returned to their ships after looting the city. Madison returned to find the mansion and all his possessions ruined. The Capitol walls remained but little else.

Madison restored order to the city. He also fired Armstrong, a move long overdue. He ordered Congress to use the Post Office and Patent Office Building for meetings,

——————————————— ✧ ———————————————

After the British swept through Washington, D.C., all that remained of the President's House (below) was an empty shell.

and he moved into a home owned by Benjamin Tayloe at New York and 18th streets. The city had been burned, but the government survived.

PEACE AT LAST

After the attack on Washington, D.C., fighting between U.S. and British forces continued. Yet Congress still failed to support the Madison administration's proposals to strengthen defenses. Monroe had asked to draft men into the army. Congress refused. Madison had great difficulty finding the money to pay the soldiers he did have. But good news finally came. In Baltimore the militia repelled a British attack. And in the South, General Andrew Jackson was successfully fighting against Native Americans who were on the side of the British.

When the British landed near New Orleans at the end of 1814, Jackson prepared to meet them. On February 4, 1815, word came of an impressive victory in New Orleans. Seven hundred British soldiers had died, and twice that number were wounded before they gave up their attack. Only seven Americans had been killed. A few days later, Madison got even better news—British and U.S. negotiators had agreed to peace at Ghent, Belgium. Madison submitted the treaty to the Senate. It ratified the treaty unanimously. The war was over.

A HERO

By going to war and standing up for U.S. rights, the American people saw Madison as a hero. In 1816 Congress went along with his proposals for new taxes, continuing the national bank, and creating a permanent navy and army.

General Jackson (above right, in white pants and holding sword), *known to his soldiers as Old Hickory, led his men to a decisive victory against the British in the Battle of New Orleans.*

———————————— ✧ ————————————

Some Republicans—and even later historians—concluded that the war had changed Madison's political ideas. They pointed out that his programs were similar to those first backed by the Federalists. But in Madison's opinion, he was simply being wise. He had always thought that a strong central government was necessary. And he was still against having a large army. But he knew firsthand that some sort of military was necessary before wartime, or other countries would be tempted to take advantage of the United States. Having a small army might do more to keep the peace than not having one at all.

The country rebounded from the War of 1812. As his term in office came to a close, Madison enjoyed himself much more. Dolley's last parties in the capital were gala affairs. Finally, the Madisons said good-bye forever to Washington, D.C., and returned to Montpelier in 1817.

RETIREMENT

In his sixties, Madison spent much of his time running the plantation. He made it a profitable and efficient business, and Jefferson called him "the best farmer in the world." He was even elected president of the local agricultural society. In the early 1820s, he survived a severe downturn in farm prices, partly because of his scientific methods. But gradually, the deepening crisis harmed even him. His finances were not helped by his stepson. Madison frequently paid off John's gambling and other debts, often to keep John from going to jail. Madison began selling off property and slaves, whom he'd once hoped to set free.

Madison did not entirely retire from politics. In 1828 he publicly countered claims that states could "nullify," or overturn, federal laws. He tried to reduce the power of slaveholding counties when

────────────── ✧

Dolley's son John was constantly in debt. No matter how much money his parents sent him, he always needed more.

Virginia revised its state constitution in 1829. He also became the rector, or head, of the University of Virginia. He succeeded Jefferson, who had founded the school and served as rector until his death on July 4, 1826.

In the winter of 1831–1832, Madison's rheumatism made him an invalid. He began spending most of his time in bed. Still, he continued to work. He sorted his papers so future generations would know what had happened during important events such as the Constitutional Convention and the War of 1812.

Dolley helped as always. "My days are devoted to nursing and comforting my sick patient," wrote Dolley in 1835, referring to her husband.

During the summer of 1836, friends suggested various cures and special medicines for his rheumatism and failing health. They all knew James Madison was dying but thought it would be a fitting end if he could at least live until July 4, America's birthday. Madison did not oblige them. He was ready to die when his time came. It arrived on the morning of June 28, 1836, while he was eating

✧ ————————————

Madison's painful arthritis confined him to his bed for much of his last five years.

breakfast with his niece Nelly Willis. She looked over and asked what was wrong.

"Nothing more than a change of mind, my dear," he said. Then his head slipped off to the side, and he died. The next day, Madison was buried in the family plot a mile away, finally at rest.

At a memorial service two months later in Boston, former president John Quincy Adams told the crowd that Madison's "small voice" still echoed through the country. His voice is still heard in the halls of Congress and on the streets, in the Supreme Court and in places of worship. Wherever Americans assert their right to freedom of religion or speech, they echo arguments James Madison once made. Whenever Americans debate the role of government in upholding those rights, they repeat the arguments Madison once used to convince a skeptical country to adopt the Constitution. Few people before Madison realized how important a strong central government was in preserving individual rights. After Madison, few doubted it.

TIMELINE

1751 James Madison is born on March 16.

1762 Madison begins his schooling.

1769 Madison goes to the College of New Jersey, later known as Princeton University.

1774 Madison is selected to the committee of safety in Orange County, Virginia. He is already a strong revolutionist.

1775 The Battles of Lexington and Concord mark the beginning of the Revolutionary War.

1776 Madison joins the Virginia General Assembly, the state's legislative body. The Continental Congress adopts the Declaration of Independence.

1778 Working first with Virginia governor Patrick Henry and then Governor Thomas Jefferson, Madison works on the Council of State.

1780 Madison joins the Continental Congress in Philadelphia.

1783 The United States and Great Britain sign the Treaty of Paris, officially ending the Revolutionary War.

1787 Madison attends the Constitutional Convention, presenting his blueprint for the Constitution known as the Virginia Plan. In September the Constitution is adopted by the convention. Madison works with Alexander Hamilton and John Jay to write the *Federalist Papers*, eloquent arguments in favor of the new plan.

1789 Madison takes a seat in the new U.S. Congress.

1790 Madison first splits with Hamilton over Hamilton's financial plans.

1792 Madison helps persuade Washington to run for a second term as president.

1796 Madison breaks with the president, criticizing him during a battle over the Jay Treaty.

1797 Madison marries Dolley Payne Todd.

1798 Madison protests the Alien and Sedition Acts.

1800 Madison helps Thomas Jefferson in his bid for president. The election ends in a tie, broken by the Federalist-controlled Congress.

1801 Thomas Jefferson appoints Madison secretary of state.

1803 Madison helps arrange the purchase of the Louisiana Territory from France.

1808 Madison runs for president and wins.

1812 Frustrated by continued British actions against U.S. shipping and sailors, Madison finally asks Congress to declare war, beginning the War of 1812. He is elected to a second term as president.

1814 A British force sets fire to Washington, D.C., but Madison, who helped direct the defense, escapes.

1815 The war ends. Though the situation between the United States and Great Britain was not changed by the peace treaty, most Americans consider the war a success.

1817 Madison leaves Washington, D.C., after two terms as president.

1826 Madison becomes rector of the University of Virginia.

1836 Madison dies at Montpelier on June 28.

SOURCE NOTES

7 James Madison, *Writings,* ed. Jack
N. Rakove (New York: The
Library of America, 1999), 682

9 Ibid., 3.

11 Irving Brant, *James Madison: The
Virginia Revolutionist*, vol. 1
(Indianapolis: The Bobbs-Merrill
Company, 1941), 33.

13 Ibid., 60.

16 Brant, *Revolutionist*, 87.

17 John Locke quoted in Brant,
Revolutionist, 84.

19 Ralph Ketcham, *James Madison:
A Biography* (Charlottesville, VA:
University Press of Virginia,
1990), 51.

21 Madison, 10.

21 Ibid., 7.

24 Brant, *Revolutionist*, 141.

24 Ibid., 144.

27 Ketcham, 71.

27 Madison, 10.

28 Ketcham, 72.

31 Ibid., 109.

33 Madison, 96.

35 Ibid., 59.

36 Ketcham, 186.

37 Madison, 80.

43 Richard B. Morris, *The Forging of
the Union, 1781–1789* (New
York: Harper & Row, 1987), 286.

43 Irving Brant, *James Madison:
Father of the Constitution* , vol. 3
(Indianapolis: The Bobbs-Merrill
Company, 1950), 123.

43 Morris, 286.

44 Brant, *Constitution*, 120.

45 Madison, 517.

50 Ketcham, 256.

50 Ibid., 258.

53 Ibid., 308.

53 Ibid.

54 Robert A. Rutland, *James
Madison: The Founding Father*
(New York: Macmillan Publishing
Company, 1987), 98.

57 Ketcham, 292.

59 Brant, *Constitution*, 356.

62 Ketcham, 376.

65 Ibid., 380.

65 Madison, 550.

66 Brant, *Constitution*, 406.

66 Ibid., 410.

67 Ibid., 417.

70 Dumas Malone, *Jefferson and the
Ordeal of Liberty* (Boston: Little,
Brown and Company, 1962),
276.

70 Madison, 581.

70 Ibid.

77 Thomas Jefferson, *Writings*, ed.
Merrill D. Peterson (New York:
The Library of America, 1984),
493–494.

78 Merrill D. Peterson, ed., *The
Portable Thomas Jefferson* (New
York: Penguin Books, 1975),
292.

79 Irving Brant, *Secretary of State,*
vol. 4 (Indianapolis: The Bobbs-
Merrill Company, 1953), 38.

83 Virginia Moore, *The Madisons*
(New York: McGraw-Hill Book
Company, 1979), 160.

87 Madison, 690

87 Ibid., 680.

92 Ketcham, 530.

92 Madison, 684.

93 Ketcham, 582.

95 Ibid., 558

96 Madison, 702.

97 Ketcham, 576.

100 Ibid., 621.

102 Ibid., 668.

103 Ibid., 670.

103 Ibid.

SELECTED BIBLIOGRAPHY

Adams, Henry. *History of the United States of America during the Administration of James Madison*. New York: The Library of America, 1986.

———. *History of the United States of America during the Administration of Thomas Jefferson*. New York: The Library of America, 1986.

Alley, Robert S., ed. *James Madison on Religious Liberty*. Buffalo: Prometheus Books, 1985.

Bailyn, Bernard. *The Debate on the Constitution: Federalist and Anti-Federalist Speeches, Articles, and Letters during the Struggle over Ratification*. 2 vols. New York: The Library of America, 1993.

Berkin, Carol. *A Brilliant Solution: Inventing the American Constitution*. New York: Harcourt, 2002.

Bowen, Catherine Drinker. *Miracle at Philadelphia: The Story of the Constitutional Convention*. Boston: Little, Brown and Company, 1966.

Cohen, I. Bernard. *Science and the Founding Fathers*. New York: W. W. Norton & Company, 1995.

Coles, Harry L. *The War of 1812*. Chicago: University of Chicago Press, 1965.

Ferling, John. *John Adams: A Life*. Knoxville, TN: University of Tennessee Press, 1992.

Hamilton, Alexander, James Madison, and John Jay. *The Federalist*. Edited by Benjamin F. Wright. 1961. Reprint, New York: Metro Books, 2002.

Jefferson, Thomas. *Writings*. Edited by Merrill D. Peterson. New York: The Library of America, 1984.

Ketcham, Ralph. *James Madison: A Biography*. Charlottesville, VA: University Press of Virginia, 1990.

Madison, James. *Writings*. Edited by Jack N. Rakove. New York: New American Library, 1999.

Mathews, Richard K. *If Men Were Angels: James Madison and the Heartless Empire of Reason*. Lawrence, KS: University Press of Kansas, 1995.

McCullough, David. *John Adams*. New York: Simon & Schuster, 2001.

Moore, Virginia. *The Madisons*. New York: McGraw-Hill Book Company, 1979.

Morison, Samuel Eliot. *The Oxford History of the American People*. New York: Oxford University Press, 1965.

Morris, Richard B. *The Forging of the Union, 1781–1789*. New York: Harper & Row, 1987.

Pole, J. R. ed. *The American Constitution, For and Against: The Federalist and Anti-Federalist Papers*. New York: Hill and Wang, 1987.

Rutland, Robert A. *James Madison: The Founding Father*. New York: Macmillan Publishing Company, 1987.

Smith, Page. *A New Age Now Begins: A People's History of the American Revolution*. 2 vols. New York: McGraw-Hill Book Company, 1976.

Washington, George. *Writings*. Edited by John Rhodehamel. New York: The Library of America, 1997.

Wills, Garry. *James Madison*. New York: Times Books/Henry Holt, 2002.

FURTHER READING, WEBSITES, AND VIDEOS

Behrman, Carol H. *Thomas Jefferson*. Minneapolis: Lerner Publications Company, 2004.

Bjornlund, Lydia. *The Constitution and the Founding of America*. San Diego: Lucent Books, 2000.

Bohannon, Lisa Frederiksen. *The American Revolution*. Lerner Publications Company, 2004.

Faber, Doris, and Harold Faber. *We the People: The Story of the United States Constitution since 1787*. New York: Charles Scribner's Sons, 1987.

Hermann, Edward, et al. *Founding Fathers*. Produced by MPH Entertainment. 200 min. A&E Television Network, 2000. Videocassette.

James Madison: His Legacy. <http://www.jmu.edu/Madison>. This is the website of the James Madison Center at James Madison University. This excellent resource has pages devoted to many different areas of Madison's life as well as the country's early history.

James Madison's Montpelier. <http://www.montpelier.org>. This is the home page of Madison's home, Montpelier. Data on Madison and his family is here, as well as information about visiting the home.

Jones, Veda Boyd. *Thomas Jefferson: Author of the Declaration of Independence*. Philadelphia: Chelsea House, 2000.

Kelley, Brent P. *James Madison: Father of the Constitution*. Philadelphia: Chelsea House, 2001.

Meisner, James. *American Revolutionaries and Founders of the Nation*. Springfield, NJ: Enslow Publishers, 1999.

Nardo, Don. *The Bill of Rights*. San Diego: Greenhaven Press, 1998.

Patrick, Jean L. S. *Dolley Madison*. Minneapolis: Lerner Publications Company, 2002.

Plfueger, Lynda. *Dolley Madison: Courageous First Lady*. Springfield, NJ: Enslow Publishers, 1999.

Roberts, Jeremy. *George Washington*. Minneapolis: Lerner Publications Company, 2003.

Swain, Gwyneth. *Declaring Freedom: A Look at the Declaration of Independence, the Bill of Rights, and the Constitution*. Minneapolis: Lerner Publications Company, 2003.

Warrick, Karen Clemens. *War of 1812: "We Have Met the Enemy and They Are Ours."* Springfield, NJ: Enslow Publishers, 2002.

INDEX

Adams, John, 55, 59, 61, 70, 72–73, 75
Adams, John Quincy, 102
Alien and Sedition Acts, 73–75
American minutemen, 26
American Whig Society, 15
Armstrong, John, 93, 96, 98
Articles of Confederation, 34, 38

Bank Bill, 54–55
Bill of Rights, 48, 52, 56–57, 74
Bonaparte, Napoleon, 81, 90, 93
Boston Tea Party, 19–20
Bradford, William, 18, 23–24
Burr, Aaron, 18, 62, 75–76, 78

Canada, 92
Chesapeake, 84, 85
Church of England, 13–15, 22
Clinton, DeWitt, 94
Clinton, George, 86
Coles, Edward, 92
College of New Jersey (Princeton), 13–19
committees of safety, 24
Congress, 28–31, 38–40, 51
Connecticut Compromise, 40, 42–43
Constitutional Convention, 35–44
Continental Congress, first, 24; second, 26, 29

Declaration of Rights, 27
democracy, 8, 44, 46, 67, 74

economy, 23, 34, 52–55, 85, 89
Embargo Act, 85, 89
Erskine, David M., 90

Federalist Papers, 46
Floyd, Catherine "Kitty," 30–31
France, 72–73, 75, 80–82, 84–85, 89–93
Freneau, Philip, 18, 55

Gage, Thomas, 25
Gallatin, Albert, 68, 79, 85
Gerry, Elbridge, 44
Great Britain, 68–70, 80–82, 84–86, 89–100

Hamilton, Alexander, 40, 45–46; as treasury secretary, 52–55, 59–61, 66, 70, 75, 78
Harrison, William Henry, 95
Henry, Patrick, 28, 49–50, 63
House, Mary, 29, 44
House of Delegates, 28
House of Representatives, 41, 68–69, 76
Hull, William, 92–93

impressment, 82, 84, 90
Independence Hall, 29

Jackson, Andrew, 99
Jay, John, 45
Jay Treaty, 68–69
Jefferson, Thomas, 28, 31, 92; as president, 76–82, 85; as secretary of state, 52–55, 59–61, 70, 74, 75

Lafayette, Marquis de, 34
Leland, John, 47–48
Lexington and Concord, Battles of, 26
Livingston, Robert, 80
Louisiana Purchase, 80–82

Maddison, John (great-great-grandfather), 9–10
Madison, Ambrose (brother), 12, 66, 72
Madison, Dolley Payne Todd, 62, 63, 71, 83–84, 97, 102; courtship with James Madison Jr., 65; as First Lady, 88, 100; first marriage, 63–64; marriage to James Madison Jr., 66; personality, 83–84, 88; War of 1812, 8, 97–98

Madison, Frances (Fanny) (sister), 12, 72
Madison, Frances Taylor
  (grandmother), 12
Madison, Francis (brother), 12
Madison, James Jr.: Bill of Rights, 52,
  56–57, 74; birth and childhood,
  11–13; Boston Tea Party, 20;
  Connecticut Compromise, 40,
  42–43; Constitutional Convention,
  35–44; Continental Congress, 29;
  courtship with Catherine "Kitty"
  Floyd, 30–31; courtship with Dolley
  Payne Todd, 62, 65; death of, 102;
  Declaration of Rights, 27; education,
  12–19; *Federalist Papers,* 46; health,
  19, 50, 78, 79, 102; as hero, 100;
  marriage to Dolley Payne Todd, 66;
  military funding, 90–92; opposition
  to slavery, 33, 43; personality of,
  83–84, 88–89; political views,
  15–17, 20, 24, 34–37, 40, 41, 44,
  48, 53–57, 60–61, 67–69, 74–75,
  87, 88, 101; Port Bill, 23–24; as
  president, 87–100; as presidential
  candidate, 85–86; religious
  philosophy, 15, 21–22, 27, 91;
  retirement, 101; as secretary of state,
  79–82, 84–85; speaking style, 41,
  44, 49–50; Virginia Convention, 27;
  Virginia Plan, 37–39; War of 1812,
  7–8, 92–100; writings of, 16, 42,
  45–46
Madison, James Sr. (father), 10–12,
  24–25, 71, 72; death of, 79
Madison, Nellie Conway (mother),
  11–12, 72
Madison, Nelly (sister), 12, 19
Madison, Sarah (sister), 12, 19
Madison, William (brother), 12, 19
Mason, George, 27, 29
Mississippi River, 80
Monroe, James, 81, 82, 97, 99
Montpelier, 12, 33, 71–72, 100–101
Moore, William (uncle), 27
Mount Vernon, 51

Nassau Hall, 14–15, 18
National Gazette, 55
New Jersey Plan, 39–40
New Orleans, Louisiana, 80–81, 99–100
Nonintercourse Act, 89–90

Parliament, 17, 23
Paterson, William, 39
Payne, Anna, 71
Perry, Oliver Hazard, 95
Pinckney, Charles, 44, 86
Port Bill, 23–24
privateers, 72

Randolph, Edmund, 37, 54
Revolutionary War: beginning of, 26;
  end of, 30; battles of, 26, 30
Robertson, Donald, 13

Shays, Daniel, 34, 44
Sherman, Roger, 40
slaves and slavery, 12, 42–43;
  Madison's views on, 33, 42–43, 101
Stamp Act, 15, 17

Tea Act, 19
Todd, John Payne (stepson), 84, 63,
  64–65, 101

Virginia Convention, 27
Virginia Plan, 37–39

War of 1812, 7–8, 92–100; end of, 100
Warren, John, 94
Washington, George, 8, 26, 28–30,
  34–37, 40–41; as president, 51, 54,
  55, 58–61, 66–70, 72
Whiskey Tax, 66–67
William and Mary College, 13, 14
Willis, Nelly, 102
Witherspoon, John, 15

XYZ Affair, 72–73

ABOUT THE AUTHOR

Jeremy Roberts is the author of many books for young readers, including biographies of Joan of Arc, George Washington, Abraham Lincoln, and Tiger Woods.

PHOTO ACKNOWLEDGMENTS

The images in this book are used with the permission of: The White House, pp. 1, 6, 7, 9, 21, 33, 45, 62, 77, 87, 96; © North Wind Picture Archives, pp. 2, 23, 26, 29 (left), 39, 40, 46, 49, 51, 76, 79, 81; Library of Virginia [Neg. A9-10097], p. 10; Peter Newark's American Pictures, pp. 11, 25, 35; Photo courtesy, Belle Grove Plantation, a National Trust Historic Site, pp. 12, 19; Collection, Princeton University Library, p. 14; Courtesy of Department of History, Presbyterian Church (USA), p. 15; Dictionary of American Portraits, p. 18 (right); Library of Congress, pp. 18 (left) [LC-USZ6-830], 20, 22 [LC-USZ62-3291], 31 [LC-USZC4-4099], 32 [LC-USZC4-4098], 38 [LC-D416-9861], 42 [LC-USZ62-70454], 48 [LC-USZ62-84448], 59 [LC-USZ62-126308], 83 (left) [LC-USZ62-16960], 90 [LC-USZ62-75535], 93 [LC-USZ62-070643], 94 [LC-USZC2-604], 98; Independence National Historical Park, p. 29 (right); Pennsylvania Department of Commerce, p. 30; National Archives, pp. 56, 100; © Bettmann/CORBIS, pp. 58, 60, 73; Virginia Historical Society, Richmond, Virgina, pp. 63, 83 (right); © Lee Snider/CORBIS, p. 64; © Art Resource, NY, p. 67; © Independent Picture Service, pp. 68, 82; © The Art Archive/Chateau de Blerancourt/Dagli Orti, p. 71; © Hulton Getty/Getty Images, p. 89; © Stock Montage, pp. 101, 102

Front cover: © Bettmann/CORBIS